THE P[illegible]
OF THE MOORS

By the same author:

The Great Teresa (Chatto and Windus 1960)
The Desert My Dwelling Place (Hodder and Stoughton 1968)
I Stay in the Church (The Vision Press 1973)
Cardinal Suenens: A Portrait (Hodder and Stoughton 1975)

Selections, with introduction, published by Darton, Longman and Todd:

Servants of Love: The Spirituality of St Teresa of Avila 1975
The Voice of the Spirit: The Spirituality of St John of the Cross 1976
The Ways of the Spirit: The Spirituality of Cardinal Suenens 1976
Your God? Cardinal Suenens's Oxford University Mission 1978

THE PRIEST OF THE MOORS

Reflections on
Nicholas Postgate

Elizabeth Hamilton

Foreword by
Cardinal Hume

Darton, Longman & Todd
London

First published in 1980 by
Darton, Longman & Todd Ltd
89 Lillie Road
London SW6 1UD

ISBN 0 232 51498 4

Grateful thanks are due to the following for permission to reproduce illustrative material:

The Abbot of Ampleforth (Fr Postgate's bone crucifix)
Mr Leo Cook (jacket photograph and the Postgate Cross)
The Bishop of Middlesbrough (book with signature)
Tindale's of Whitby (wood carving of Fr Postgate)

British Library Cataloguing in Publication Data

Hamilton, Elizabeth, *b. 1906*
The priest of the moors.
1. Postgate, Nicholas
2. Catholic Church – Biography
I. Title
280'.2'092

ISBN 0–232–51498–4

Phototypeset by
Input Typesetting Ltd., London SW19 8DR
Printed in Great Britain by
The Anchor Press Ltd
and bound by Wm. Brendon and Son Ltd
both of Tiptree, Essex

CONTENTS

Map of the Yorkshire of Nicholas Postgate vi–vii

Acknowledgements viii

Foreword ix

1 Setting the Scene 1

2 The Postgate Country 10

3 Missionary Priest 22

4 The Moors 32

5 The Apostolate of the Moors 44

6 The Beginning of the End 55

7 The Climax 62

8 The Postgate Tradition 73

Index of Place Names 86

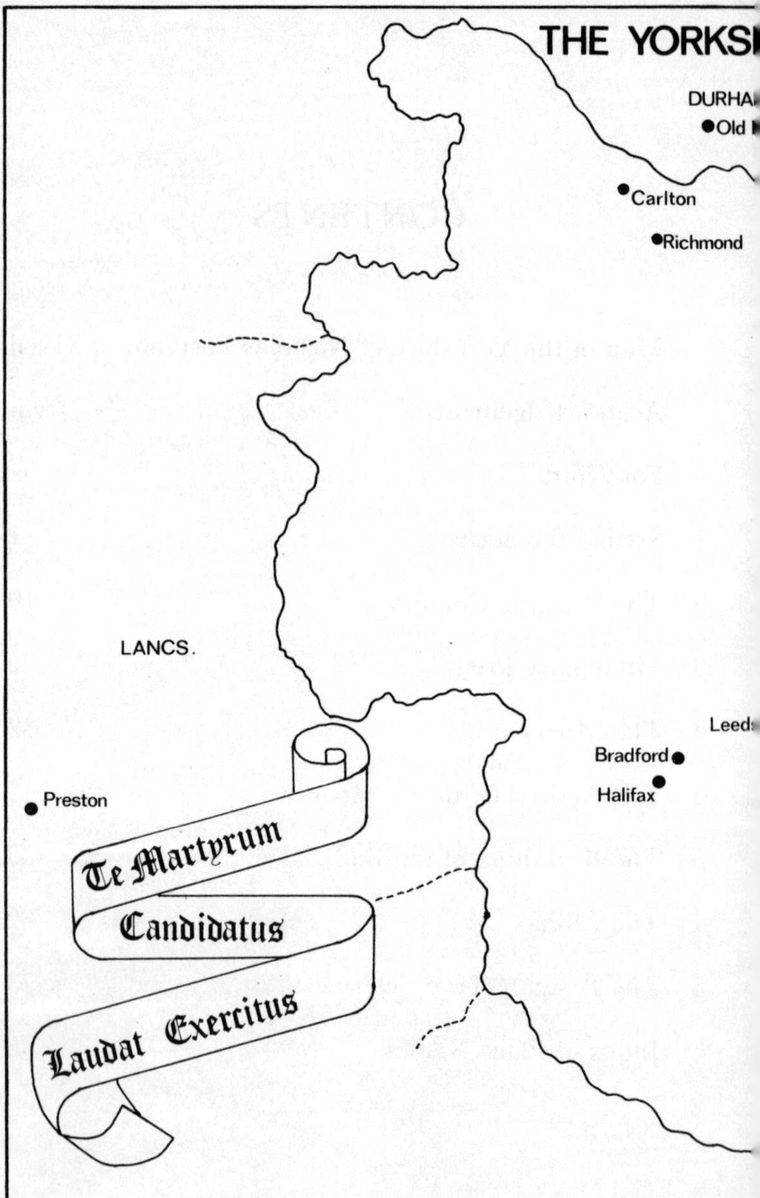

Carlton
Richmond
LANCS.
Bradford
Halifax
Preston
Te Martyrum
Candidatus
Laudat Exercitus

E OF NICHOLAS POSTGATE

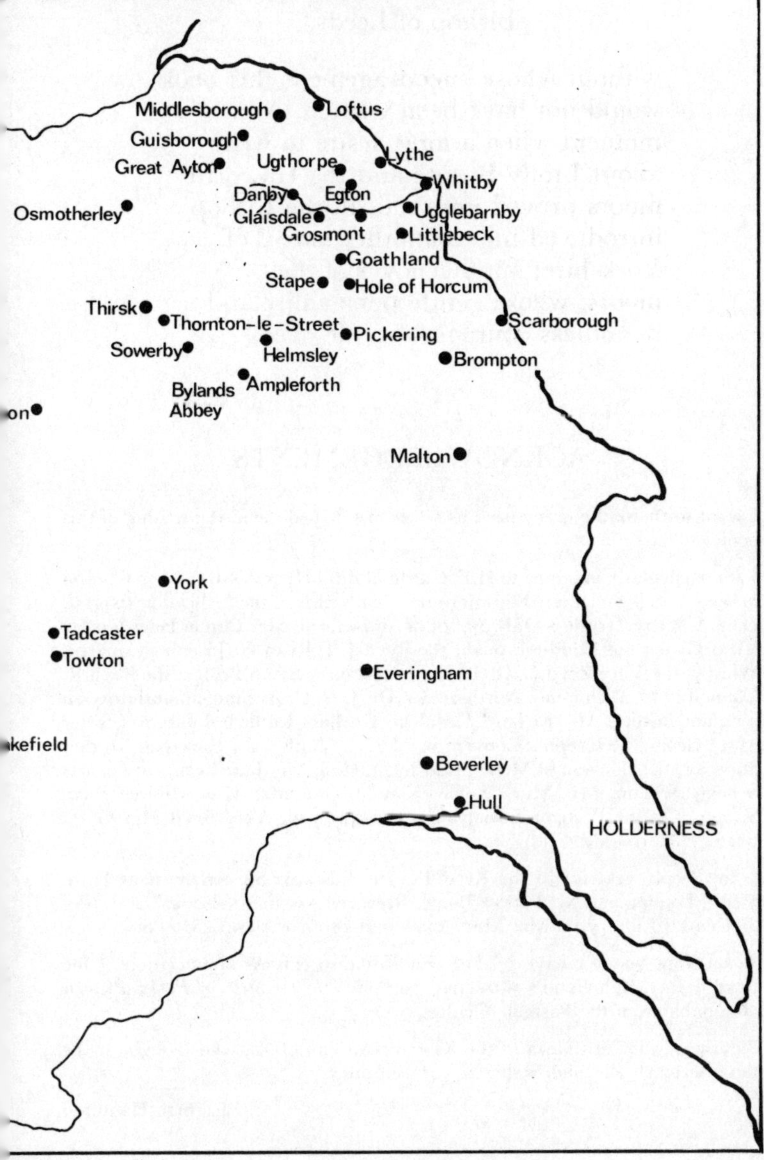

For
the Rt Revd Wm. Gordon Wheeler, M.A.
Bishop of Leeds,

without whose encouragement this book would not have been written. At a moment when a long desire to write about Emily Brontë and the Haworth moors proved impractical, the Bishop introduced me to another native of Yorkshire, another lover of the moors, whose gentle personality and boundless courage won me over.

ACKNOWLEDGEMENTS

I want to thank the many persons who have helped me in the writing of this book.

I am particularly indebted to H.E. Cardinal Basil Hume OSB; Bishop Gordon Wheeler, who contributed far more than the words of the dedication suggest; Dom Ambrose Griffiths OSB, Abbot of Ampleforth; Mgr Canon Peter Storey, Vicar General of Middlesbrough; the Revd J. J. Ryan, St Joseph's Convent, Whitby; the Very Revd C. C. Toner, St Hedda's, Egton Bridge; the Revd R. Connolly SM, Richmond, North Yorks; Dr. J. C. H. Aveling, an authority on recusant history; Mr. Richard Kornicki, Durham Cathedral Library; Sister Mary Cecily, St Joseph's Convent of Mercy, Whitby; the Reverend Mother Superior, the Convent of Mercy, Endsleigh, Hull; Mrs Jane Lecky, St Francis School, Acklam; Mrs Mary Noble, Kendal, Cumbria; Miss Mildred Raw, Secretary of the Postgate Society, Egton Bridge; the Very Revd Mgr G. T. Bradley, Harrogate.

I am deeply grateful to the Revd Francis Edwards SJ, Archivist at Farm Street, London and Mr Patrick Barry, Research Assistant; also, at the Catholic Central Library, to Mrs Mary Buck and Brother Alan LeMay SA.

Apart from books I have read, I would like to express appreciation of the Revd John Mulholland's attractive pamphlet *In the Steps of Father Postgate* obtainable from the Postgate Centre.

Finally, a word of thanks to the Revd Fr Anselm ODC, who though, at the time, seriously ill, made valuable contributions.

Elizabeth Hamilton

FOREWORD

No Roman Catholic from what used to be known as the North Riding of Yorkshire can be unaware of Nicholas Postgate, the priest who was martyred at York on 7 August 1679. Three hundred years have not obliterated his memory or destroyed the *cultus* which began on the day of his execution and has grown ever since. He has long been one of my own favourites.

Nicholas Postgate was a secular priest from Douai who came back to his native Yorkshire in 1630 and, after acting as chaplain to various local Catholic gentry for some years, spent the last twenty years or so of his life ministering to the poor Catholics who lived on the moors. Although he lived under the penal laws, his was not a life marked by thrilling escapes from pursuivants, nor one which produced any major written works, nor any similar claims to fame. He appears to have been careful not to draw attention to himself, as was prudent. He did not seek martyrdom, but pursued his priestly life in imitation of Christ by living in poverty and simplicity and by serving the poor. 'His purpose was to bring back, as far as was in his power, the Faith to England, and the Mass to the people.' In all this he provides a model of the priesthood which remains an inspiration today to all Middlesbrough priests, and one which, in all essentials, can be imitated – hardworking, unobtrusive, devoted, 'ordinary' – except in the manner of his dying.

Elizabeth Hamilton has caught the particular nuance of his spirit in this book, and has produced something of the atmosphere which prevailed in the Yorkshire of Postgate's days, when the Catholic Church was an 'underground' one in many senses. She underlines the Catholicism of the recusant families, the heavy price they paid to maintain their religious beliefs and practices and their tremendous contribution to the preservation of Catholicism in England. These pages tell us something, too, of the spirit of Catholic Yorkshire today – a spirit which owes much to Nicholas Postgate and his fellow priests who 'tramped the moors' to bring the Mass to the people, and who died for it.

Cardinal Basil Hume
Archbishop of Westminister

1

SETTING THE SCENE

The Old Mass House

In north Yorkshire as the road running south-west from Whitby drops at Egton (the 'place of the oaks') before plunging into the peaceful tree-shadowed valley of the Esk at Egton Bridge where the wild daffodils grow, you come on the left-hand side to what is called the Old Mass House. It is a small building with a tiled roof over an upstairs floor – in front, a garden, a hedge and a wooden gate. It stands high above the road on an incline known as Brown Hill from which on a clear day there is a breathtaking view extending for miles over Eskdale to the village of Grosmont, Glaisdale, the Goathland Moors, and, downstream, to Sleights. Formerly the roof was thatched, the only 'upstairs' being the space immediately below the thatch.

One day in about the year 1830 a girl was standing on a ladder cleaning the kitchen wall of the house which, until the 1920s, occupied the site of the one just mentioned, when suddenly, under the pressure of her hand, the plaster high on the wall gave way. She saw before her a small, dark loft in which there was an altar prepared for the celebration of Mass. On it was a crucifix, two candlesticks, a missal, and vestments laid out. All was in readiness. Only the celebrant was missing: Nicholas Postgate (or Postgayt, or Poskate, or Poskett) had died a martyr on 7 August in the year 1679, at the Knavesmire, outside the walls of York. It was a particularly horrible death; he was hanged, drawn (disembowelled) and quartered. And he was over eighty years old.

But first, the name.

The 'locals', I am told on the highest authority, always talk of 'Father' Postgate: 'They never refer to him as Nicholas Postgate, or Postgate, or the Venerable (as he is entitled to be called) Nicholas Postgate and they won't like a book that does!' I am sorry, for I happen to like his name as it is: both the sound, and his signature as written on the flyleaf of a book in St Hedda's Church, Egton Bridge, in his own bold, Italic hand: *Nicholaus Postgayt.* True, his friend and contemporary Thomas Ward refers to him in his poem as 'Father' Postgate, but as a term of affection, endearment – in a period when the word 'Father' was not yet used as a clerical prefix.

The death of Nicholas Postgate when viewed against an historical background of roughly a century and a half is seen to have an inevitability, a logicality, reminiscent of a Greek tragedy. And yet this is not a tragedy. The victim or 'hero', as he is more often called, of a classical tragedy is, as Aristotle is at pains to make clear, 'a good man', better than we are, who nevertheless through a 'flaw in his character' brings about his own downfall.

Nicholas Postgate was a good man, better than most of us can hope to be. If he had a flaw or defect of character – and who to some degree has not? – there is no evidence that this had anything to do with his downfall. Nor is 'downfall' the right word. Victory would be more appropriate.

Possibly an incident from real life might help to clarify this point. A professor of Greek, while reflecting with his students upon situations taken, some from literature, some from life, was asking whether this one or that was fundamentally a tragedy. 'Christ crucified?' he went on, 'Was that a tragedy?' Then, without waiting, he replied to his own question: 'No. Not, at least, according to Christian premises. Christ was not the victim of a character defect; he was in charge of a situation which he had accepted in complete freedom of will. He was victorious.' The professor was an agnostic.

Nicholas Postgate was not Jesus Christ, but he walked in his footsteps. Not to feel compassion for Postgate's sufferings would be less than human. But compassion is not enough. We owe it to him to understand, at least in the main, the events which led up to his martyrdom.

Queen Elizabeth I (1558–1603)

Nicholas Postgate *alias* Whitmore, Whitemore, Whitemoor or Watson, died in the reign of Charles II. But to understand, we must go back to Henry VIII: to the year 1534 when by an Act of Parliament Henry became Supreme Head of the Church in England. Then in 1559, by another Act of Parliament, Elizabeth I, who had succeeded her Catholic half-sister, Mary Tudor, became 'the only Supreme governor of this realm . . . as well in all spiritual or ecclesiastical things or causes as temporal'. Like her father, she was head of the Church in England as well as of the State. This was bolstered up by an Act of Uniformity reauthorising the use of Edward VI's *Book of Common Prayer* (1552), thus imposing once more the Protestant form of worship. Bishops who refused to take the new Oath of Supremacy were deprived of their sees, clergy who would not use the *Book of Common Prayer* were fined or imprisoned, and the laity, if they did not attend a Protestant service in their parish church on Sunday, were fined.

Later, the penalties were increased and the new order enforced more stringently. Some, refusing to submit, went into hiding or exile. Many conformed, at least outwardly, which for the moment was enough. Many continued to practise their Faith in secret. For a while there was little persecution.

Then, several factors caused the situation to worsen. In 1569 there was the Northern Rising. It was an attempt led by the Earls of Northumberland and Westmorland to secure toleration for Catholics and freedom for Mary Queen of Scots (cousin of Elizabeth and a prisoner for the last year at Bolton Castle) whom Catholics looked upon as the rightful heir to the English throne. The rising failed and many involved were put to death.

Then in February 1570 Pope Pius V in the bull *Regnans in excelsis* excommunicated Elizabeth with the predictable result that an English Catholic was *ipso facto* suspected of disloyalty to the Queen. The penal laws were consequently enforced more severely. Suspicion against Catholics was further heightened by the arrival in 1574 of the first missionary priests from the English College at Douai, in Flanders, founded in 1568 for the training of secular clergy. In 1580, Jesuits too began to arrive and, before the close of the reign, newly ordained priests from various seminaries founded at Rome in 1579, Valladolid in 1589, Seville in 1592 and, later, Lisbon in 1627.

The impact made by this influx of mission priests was such that a statute was introduced in 1581 making reconciliation with the Catholic Church high treason. This was followed by the most harsh of the penal laws, the one particularly relevant to Nicholas Postgate: the statute of 1585 (27 Elizabeth 1.2) 'against Jesuits, seminary priests, and such other like disobedient persons'. Priests ordained on the Continent were ordered to leave England within forty days. Those who remained behind and did not take the Oath of Supremacy in three days, would be guilty of treason. Anyone who sheltered or maintained such a person, would be guilty of felony. Both offences were punishable by death, the former by hanging, drawing and quartering, the latter by hanging only.

Finally there was the Spanish Armada in 1588; it was the ultimate proof in the eyes of Protestants that the Pope and Philip II of Spain were in league with the English Catholics of whom the most pernicious were the priests.

The first seminary priest to suffer the penalty of high treason was Cuthbert Mayne in the year 1577, at Launceston, Cornwall; copies of a papal bull of jubilee were found on his person. During the twenty-six years, between then and the death of Elizabeth in 1603, 183 Catholics were executed of whom 123 were priests, one a friar not yet ordained, and fifty-nine lay persons. The majority of the priests were missioners trained in seminaries on the Continent. The greater number were put to death in London, at Tyburn, and forty at York.

Catholics have reason today to be proud of the many who, under Elizabeth, gave their lives for the Faith – as well as the many others who died under the Stuarts and during the Civil War, down to Oliver Plunket, Archbishop of Armagh, executed in 1681. Yet, lest pride degenerate into complacency, it is well to recall that, in the four years under the Catholic Mary Tudor, something like 273 Protestants were burnt at the stake.

James I (1603–1625)

In 1603 James VI of Scotland, son of Mary Queen of Scots, became James I of England. He seemed at first well disposed towards Catholics. Then in 1605 came the Gunpowder Plot, an attempt to blow up the Houses of Parliament in which Catholics were implicated. The penal laws were therefore revived and, by a statute of 1606 a fresh oath of allegiance, framed in language particularly hostile to the Pope, could be demanded of anyone suspected of not attending the services of the State Church.

Later, negotiations for the marriage of the King's son and heir, Charles (later Charles I), to a Catholic princess, first the Infanta Maria of Spain, then Henrietta Maria of France, whom Charles in fact married in 1625 shortly after he became King, led to some degree of toleration and hopes for a better future.

Charles I (1625–1649)

Charles I, who succeeded his father in 1625, was by no means ill-disposed towards Catholics. His French Queen had, by the terms of the marriage treaty, an establishment of Catholic priests; the chapels of Catholic ambassadors were well attended; religious houses and schools founded on the Continent by Catholic exiles from England were prospering; Papal agents accredited to the Queen lived in London, and, by favour of the King, penal laws were in abeyance.

Until the Long Parliament forced the King's hand, two Catholics only were executed (that was in 1628): Edmund Arrowsmith, S. J., a priest, at Lancaster, and Richard Herst, a layman, also at Lancaster. Charles realized that his throne was threatened less by Catholics than by the Puritans who were predominant in Parliament; while Catholics knew that their enemy was not the King but these same Puritans.

When the Parliamentarians challenged the King's authority, persecution returned. Two priests were executed in 1641: William Ward at Tyburn, London, and Ambrose Barlow at Lancaster. Then, several others in the first half of 1642.

The Civil War and the Commonwealth (1642–1660)

During the Civil War (1642–9) the Catholics were staunch loyalists. In Yorkshire, Mrs Waterton held the family seat, Walton Hall, near Wakefield, against an assault by Parliamentarians. In 1662 Lord Fairfax wrote: 'I hear that, in York, Mass is ordinarily said in every street.' There were no prolonged persecutions. Two priests, however, were put to death: Peter Wright, a Jesuit, in 1651, and John Southworth in 1654. The judge wanted Southworth to plead 'not guilty' to the charge of being a priest. He refused; he could not do so, he said, in conscience. His body, buried at Douai, is now in Westminster Cathedral, clothed in crimson Roman vestments, a black velvet cap and shoes, his face and slender hands encased in silver.

Charles II (1660–1685)

The restoration of the monarchy in the person of Charles II in 1660 brought hope to English Catholics. The king was grateful to them for having supported the royal cause during the Civil War and for having helped him to escape to France. Moreover during his exile he had come into contact with English Catholics on the Continent. Then in 1662 he married the Catholic Catherine of Braganza, daughter of the King of Portugal. He was, in general, well disposed towards Catholics, anxious to make things easier for them in England. In the secret Treaty of Dover, made with the French in 1670, he agreed *inter alia* – in return for financial help from Louis XIV – to declare himself a Catholic when a suitable opportunity presented itself; he did so on his death-bed.

In 1672, by his Declaration of Indulgence, he suspended the penal laws against Catholics and all nonconformists. The following year, however, he was forced to go back on this, under pressure from Parliament. The Civil War and the Commonwealth had weakened his royal power; he had to give way to a Parliament which was mainly anti-Catholic.

James, Duke of York, brother of Charles and heir presumptive to the throne, became a Catholic in about the year 1669. Then, after the death of his first wife (Anne Hyde who had herself died a Catholic in 1671), he married the Catholic Mary of Modena in 1673. This was too much! The prospect of a Catholic King could not be ruled out. In the same year Parliament passed the Test Act which excluded from holding public office all who refused to take Communion in the State Church. Protestant opposition to the King was growing.

Titus Oates

The major crisis of the reign, however, was precipitated by the Oates Plot (or the Popish Plot) of 1678, when Titus Oates, a scruffy, dissolute, villainous renegade with a voice like the bleating of a sheep, gave perjured testimony about a Catholic conspiracy to massacre Protestants, to assassinate Charles and put on the throne James, the Catholic brother of Charles, the heir apparent.

The son of a Protestant clergyman, Oates studied at Cambridge, but without obtaining a degree, and took Holy Orders in 1670. Seven years later he became, or pretended to become, a Catholic. He was supported by Israel Tonge, a Protestant cleric, and by William Bedloe, an informer. He was encouraged, too, by Sir Anthony Ashley Cooper, 1st Earl of Shaftesbury. The 'Oates' of Yorkshire was Robert Bolron, formerly a collier manager of Sir Thomas Gascoigne, a wealthy West Riding baronet. Among those he betrayed on false evidence was Thomas Thwing from the North Riding, a priest who was arrested in York, condemned for treason and executed in 1680.

The outcome of the Oates Plot was a fierce persecution of Catholics. It was the last persecution in England in which Catholics, as such, were put to death. Between 1678 and 1681, Oliver Plunket, Archbishop of Armagh, eighteen priests, a Benedictine brother and six laymen were executed. Also a number of priests died in prison. The laymen and some of the priests were condemned on charges of being involved in the alleged plot. The rest of the priests were condemned under the statute of 1585 (27 Elizabeth 1.2) which forbade a Catholic priest to be on English soil. Nicholas Postgate was among these.

2

THE POSTGATE COUNTRY

In the Mass House at Egton, the oratory, concealed by the deep thatch, and the altar ready for Mass symbolized, indeed epitomized, all that the name Nicholas Postgate has stood for: his life, his death, the veneration accorded him down three centuries in his native Yorkshire by rich and poor, old and young, Catholics and non-Catholics.

In an age and in a milieu in which to be a Catholic priest in England was, in accordance with the penal laws, to be guilty of high treason, Postgate's prime objective was to serve God as a priest, care for God's people and bring the Mass to those deprived of it. His last words remind us – should a reminder be necessary – that he died not through involvement in the plot 'cooked up' by Titus Oates and his gang nor through any political entanglement, but solely, as he said, for his religion; solely, that is, because he was faithful to his calling to the priesthood.

If you continue from the Mass House, in a southerly direction, down the steep bending road and then on under the railway bridge, you will see immediately on the right-hand side, in the village of Egton Bridge, a Roman Catholic church dedicated to St Hedda, a monk of Whitby Abbey who later became Bishop of the West Saxons (his see was at Dorchester) and Bishop of Winchester; he died in 705. The centenary of the opening of this church was held in 1967. For its existence and the meticulous care with which it was looked after, we are largely indebted to the late Canon Francis Callebert, a Belgian priest who passed some forty years of his ministry in this remote 'Postgate' area, the people of which were renowned during penal times for their stubborn loyalty to the Faith. After the Catholic Relief Act of 1790 allowed Catholics to have once more their own places of worship, the Egton community under the leadership of the Revd Thomas Talbot opened a chapel in 1798. It is now the primary school.

A condition had been laid down in the Act that a Catholic chapel or the equivalent should have no steeple or bell. In 1836 Fr Greenhalgh, the priest at that time, trusting perhaps to the greater freedom being granted to Catholics as a result of the Emancipation Act of 1828, added a turret but not a bell. Even this was too much! 'The Pope of Rome has raised his head again in Egton Bridge,' the Anglican Vicar is reputed to have proclaimed. Later a bell was added which is there today.

Associations with Nicholas Postgate and Egton's reputation for loyalty dispose one to think of the district as primarily a paradise of devout Catholics, steadfast in the face of persecution, undaunted by penal laws. There is indeed truth in this, but it is not the whole truth. In the late 1660s and early 1700s its people acquired a reputation for credulity, dissent, unbelief in many forms, a suitable refuge for priests who 'blot their copy books' and laity in search of a place to hide their heads.

I cannot, in a book so deeply concerned with martyrdom, pass over Egton without recalling that, along with Glaisdale and Goathland, it was one of the chapelries of Lythe, the Vicar of which was St John Fisher, born in Beverley, and later Bishop of Rochester. He was executed under Henry VIII because he would not acknowledge the King as the Supreme Head of the Church in England.

Kirkdale House

Beyond St Hedda's Church pass a turning to the right. Then, further on, the road on which you are walking turns sharply right across Egton Bridge, once made of stone, now, since the River Esk floods of 1930, iron. Immediately beyond the bridge, on the left, lie buried the foundations of Kirkdale House.

The name, Kirkdale House, is imposing. However, such evidence as we have suggests a small building. The late Fr David Quinlan, writing in 1967, mentions 'persons still living' who recall the remains of the house as being, in their childhood, 'knee-high', and how, after Mass in St Hedda's, children would play among the ruins, jumping over walls into and out of the building. Others are quoted as saying the walls were two or three feet high. Someone else describes the house as no better than a cattle shed. On the other hand, J. C. H. Aveling, an authority on this period, gives, in *Northern Catholics* (1966), the home of Nicholas Postgate as Dean Hall near Ugglebarnby, about five miles from Whitby, and describes Nicholas as the son of a prosperous farmer.

Boyhood

However, Kirkdale House at Egton Bridge is generally assumed to be the place where Nicholas Postgate was born about the year 1600. There are some discrepancies as to dates. According to the third *Douai Diary* he was twenty-one when he entered the English College at Douai, in Flanders, in 1621 to study for the priesthood. Bishop Challoner, on the other hand, says he was born 'about the end of the sixteenth century'. The year 1599 is sometimes given. Again, as to his age when he died in 1679, there are slight variations: 'about ninety'; 'over eighty'; 'aged eighty-two'; 'full four score and three';

'eighty and three times one'. The parish registers at Egton go back only to 1622.

The son of James and Margaret Postgate (née Watson), Nicholas came of a family, the *Douai Diary* affirms, that had suffered much for the Faith; *parentes plurima passi sunt pro fide Catholica*, which means that apart from anything else, they had paid heavy fines for being recusants – that is to say, for having remained faithful to the Catholic Church.

But fines were only one problem. The most serious was the shortage of priests, and this was being dealt with by the introduction of missionaries – young men trained on the Continent and then brought back to their own country where the need for them was great. In England, Catholic practices were dropping out more and more: the Latin Mass; the saying of Office; the Rosary; penance; praying to Our Lady and the Saints; the keeping of feast days; the lighting of candles. At Leeds, Catholic books, vestments, crucifixes were among objects defaced and sold to raise money for the poor. In a roof in the Swine Market in Wakefield were found hidden a quantity of painted wooden and alabaster statues representing saints.

James Postgate died in 1602, leaving Margaret to bring up three sons: Matthew, William and Nicholas. William, who later lived in Oxfordshire, became the father of Ralph Postgate, a distinguished Jesuit born in 1648 and twice Rector of the Venerable English College in Rome. Margaret died in 1624, by which time Nicholas had gone to Douai. She left the family property to Matthew, the eldest.

It is tempting and not unrealistic (it fits in with the occasional mentions of Postgate's liking for music) to accept the tradition that this Nicholas Postgate is one and the same as an adolescent of that name who in January 1616 was fined ten shillings at the Quarter Sessions at Helmsley in the North Riding. The boy described as a thirteen-year-old labourer from Egton was one of eight strolling players wandering around begging: '*communes histriones vagabundi et mendici*', the indictment says somewhat scornfully. What were known as the Egton Interlude Players or the Simpson Players were said to be popular by reason of their mocking allusions to the State and to the Established Church. One Interlude comprised a dialogue between a priest and a parson, ending with the parson being carried off to hell by the devil! There was, 'much popery and much abuse of law and justice'. Some say these entertainments were popular at Douai and may have been introduced, or at any rate encouraged, by missionary priests from there.

Whether or not Nicholas Postgate was one of these players is uncertain. However, it is certain that on 4 July 1621 he entered the English College at Douai accompanied by Francis Greene, a priest of the College, and two brothers from Yorkshire, Thomas and John Tankard. At Douai Nicholas assumed the name of Whitmore, using various spellings. It was normal for a student to use an *alias* to avoid the possibility, were he to be called by his own name, of bringing trouble on his family or benefactors, since it was a penal offence for Catholics to be educated outside England.

Whitmore? Whitemoor? White moor? The third spelling probably tells us most. Nicholas's home at Egton Bridge lay in a valley below the sombre, Brontëish expanse of moorland, known then and still today as 'Blackamoor' – Black moor. The choice of the name 'White moor' is in line with a wry, unobtrusive touch of humour that is part of Postgate's make-up.

He entered Douai, the *Diary* records, as an *alumnus*, and in return for his education and keep he would contribute the sum of 300 florins: *pro summa trecentorum florenorum pro alumno admittitur*. The Tankard brothers on the other hand entered as *convictores*. In principle an *alumnus* was educated free, at the expense, that is, of the

College. A *convictor* payed his own expenses – often in England in advance through an agent representing the College. The system, however, was not always rigid. Financially Douai was extremely badly off. Sometimes young men had to be turned away because there was not the money to keep them. Contributions were welcomed from a number of sources, including the Vatican, King Philip II of Spain and other benefactors. Circumstances being such, *alumni* sometimes gave offerings according to their means; Nicholas Postgate was one of these. If the system was not unduly rigid, nor was the usage of words. Occasionally the same person is referred to now as an *alumnus*, now as a *convictor*. Dom Bede Camm says Nicholas was a '*convictor* not an ordinary student because he was already a man'.

Douai

Douai used to be called 'the mother and nurse' of the English martyrs. The first to be executed, as we have noted, was Cuthbert Mayne in 1577, at Launceston; the last, Thomas Thwing at York in 1680. The College had been founded in 1568 by Dr William Allen, later Cardinal, a native of the county of Lancaster who, as a recusant, was exiled from Oxford where he had been Master of St Mary's Hall. His aim at Douai had been to train, with the aid of some Fellows from Oxford, spiritually minded, well-educated secular priests in readiness for the day when the accession of a Catholic sovereign would once more restore the Faith to England. Then, feeling that to wait indefinitely would be unrealistic, he decided to smuggle across the Channel clergy capable of participating in a secret mission along with the hardships this would entail.

Dr Allen attached less importance to formal regulations than to mutual charity and apostolic zeal. But he knew that a disciplined spiritual life was necessary. The day began with Mass at 5 a.m. in the chapel dedicated to St Thomas of Canterbury; those not yet ordained received Holy Communion, and Divine Office was said by all. Confession was no longer, as it had tended to become, a perfunctory yearly obligation. Life in the College was far from luxurious: the buildings were often in bad repair, the furniture sparse, the food no more than adequate. What mattered, in Dr Allen's view, was that the seminarians should be enured to face, for the sake of Christ and his Church, privation, discomfort, danger, imprisonment and, if need be, martyrdom.

Academically the emphasis was on theology, philosophy, and the Scriptures. Theology was taught by the President and an assistant, logic by several professors. There are references to Greek classes. Hebrew, too, is mentioned. Latin was not limited to ecclesiastical writers: classical works mentioned include Cicero's *Epistulae*, *De Amicitia*, *De Senectute*; Caesar's *De Bello Gallico*; Virgil's *Aeneid VI* and *XII*, his *Georgics* and *Bucolics*. Much time was devoted to studying and reading aloud the Old Testament and the New. Each Sunday and Feast Day a student gave a homily. In 1648 French was added to the curriculum. Dramatic performances on sacred and historical themes were popular, the *libretti* usually written in Latin verse.

Mission Priests

In 1573 the first four priests were ordained at Douai. In 1574 the first four sailed for England. By 1578 (in which year the College had to move temporarily to Rheims where it remained till 1593) seventy-five priests had been ordained and fifty-two sent to England. That was only the beginning.

To these mission priests, English Catholics owe an

incalculable debt. A. O. Meyer, the Lutheran authority, in *England and the Catholic Church under Queen Elizabeth*, writes: 'In no other European country at the time of the Counter-Reformation did the Catholic Church possess a clergy who discharged their priestly duties with such a holy zeal as the little band that worked in England.'

That is not to say that none apostatized. It is not to say they were flawless. But neither were the twelve Apostles. Joseph Berington, himself a priest – Aveling calls him a 'clerical *enfant terrible*' – gives his impressions of the Douai clergy in a book written between 1780 and 1781, *The State and Behaviour of English Catholics*. What he says – if I am not misled by the somewhat archaic language – is roughly as follows: 'The priests from Douai are open, singleminded, devout, hardworking, to be relied upon in carrying out their duties, dedicated to their calling, eager to be faithful to the tradition of those gone before. On the other hand they are sometimes harsh in applying the principles by which they live, narrow in outlook, ignorant of the ways of the world and, it must be confessed, "unpleasant in their manners".' It is fair to add that the shortcomings listed above, Berington makes clear, are not peculiar to the clergy of Douai.

Martyrs

They were therefore mostly ordinary men. But among them were those (more numerous probably than we can ever know) who, when the moment presented itself, were capable of rising above the ordinary – capable of facing imprisonment, exile, excruciating torment, death. And what, one may ask, enabled them to do so? The grace of the Holy Spirit working within each one, enabling each one to draw to the full upon his human qualities whether these were inborn or fostered by example and education – be it courage, fortitude, faith, a tranquil heart, an appreciation of the dignity of man and, not least, a sense of humour which time and again dumbfounded those who witnessed their death. 'They laugh, they cannot fear death!' the crowd exclaimed as they watched Edmund Campion and his companions being dragged to the gallows.

Campion was at Douai in 1572 and received there Minor Orders, the Subdiaconate. In 1573 he entered the Jesuit seminary at Rome. The spirit in the different continental seminaries was fundamentally one and the same. It echoed the gaiety with which Thomas More had gone to his death, a jest upon his lips, reminding friends and family that all this was passing, that they would be together in heaven, rejoicing 'full merrily'. Or think of Oliver Plunket, roughly a century and a half later, who spoke of his approaching execution as 'a mere flea-byte'.

Nor must I leave out Alban Roe, the 'black sheep'. Having studied at Cambridge he entered the seminary at Douai, only to be expelled. His contempt for discipline, his Superiors complained, was totally unacceptable. Not only that, he led others astray. That was in 1610. Then the Benedictines took him on. Ordained a priest in 1615, he died a martyr at Tyburn in 1642. Having tipped the hangman and warned him not to get drunk, he said on the scaffold: 'I wish I had a thousand lives to sacrifice for a cause so worthy!'

Among the martyrs of those times it became a tradition, a matter of *esprit de corps*, to face death with a dignity and lightness of heart that baffled – indeed put to shame – those who witnessed their end, gave courage too, to their fellow sufferers.

A whole book could be devoted to this subject. I will merely take at random four more who were trained for the priesthood at Douai, or at Rheims during the time when the English College was temporarily based in that city.

In 1586 when Francis Ingleby was executed at York, his Puritan goaler was so moved by the prisoner's 'sweet and joyous conversation' that he could not keep back his tears.

When George Napier (or Napper) was in prison in Oxford in 1610 waiting to be told the day of his execution, he invited, to while away the time, a couple of men less well off than himself to enjoy with him a supper of roast mutton provided by a friend. Then, as the days dragged on, his appetite, not surprisingly, went off, so that he could eat only 'a piece of pigeon pie and a few prunes'. When, however, news came that he was to die, he decked himself in fresh apparel – white waistcoat, white stockings, white breeches – and, embracing his executioner, gave him 'for his trouble' a silver piece embossed with a figure of St George.

In August 1679, when the ninety-year-old John Wall was executed, a fortnight after Postgate, on Red Hill overlooking the city of Worcester, the Protestant onlookers could feel only sympathy and admiration at the courage and the cheerfulness with which the old man faced his end.

On the same day at Hereford John Kemble, before going to the gallows, calmly smoked a last pipe of tobacco with the Under-Sherriff, Mr Humphrey Digges. Never, said the Protestants who witnessed his martyrdom, had they seen anyone die 'so like a gentleman, so like a Christian'.

Many too were the martyrs who, accused of disloyalty and disobedience to their Sovereign, prayed as they went to their death for this same Sovereign, for his (or her) welfare in this world and in the world to come. Napier prayed for the King, for the prince and all the royal children. Then he prayed again, saying: 'I pray God bless his Majesty and make him a saint in heaven.' Edmund Campion the Jesuit had prayed for Elizabeth I, then added: 'A day will come, Elizabeth, that will show thee plainly who loved thee best, the Society of Jesus or Luther's brood.'

So striking is the humour, vivacity, cheerfulness and gaiety displayed by these men and others of their kind that one cannot but ask whether they were supported by the grace of the Holy Spirit in the general sense whereby anyone who asks in faith is granted the strength to endure the seemingly unendurable. Or have we here the bestowal of that unique grace bought by Christ, the Word made Flesh, when he chose to endure for us men and our salvation not only the physical anguish of all that a crucifixion entails, but the indignity of being blindfolded, scourged, spat upon, mocked – this, and, crowning all, the agony of knowing that as he hung upon the Cross, in loneliness and abandonment, his Mother was standing there at his side, witnessing his final dereliction?

Let us recall, too, that there were those who did not attain the glory of martyrdom. They were left to die in prison, their 'biography' comprising no more than a line or two in the *Douai Diaries*. William Allison, we read, died in prison in York in 1679 or 1680. That is all we know. And the name could be an *alias*.

On 16 September 1627, approximately six years after entering Douai, Nicholas Postgate, having followed the normal courses and taken the College oaths, sat for the examination that preceded the reception of Minor Orders. He was ordained Subdeacon on 18 December 1627, Deacon on 18 March 1628, then Priest on 20 March – the three Orders being conferred at Arras by the Most Revd Paul Baudot, Archbishop of that See. He sang his first Mass on 2 April. For the knowledge that he sang his Mass, we are indebted to notes made by John Knaresborough, a Yorkshire priest who took the greatest interest in all that concerned Nicholas Postgate; these notes Knaresborough called *Foule Draughtes* or 'Rough Notes'.

On 23 October 1627, we read in the *Diary*, he had been sacristan of the College: *Mr Nicholas Whitemore curam suscepit vestarii.* He carried out his duties, the *Diary* records in a later entry, *magna cum fidelitate, diligentia ac Collegii emolumento.* In other words, he had worked hard and given the College good service.

Twenty-one (the age at about which Nicholas Postgate entered Douai) was considered, at that time, late to enter a seminary. Postgate had a sense of responsibility; he knew precisely what he was doing. His purpose was to bring back, as far as was in his power, the Faith to England, the Mass to the people. Having lived from childhood under the penal laws he knew what to expect. He knew all about recusants – his family were such. He knew the lot of priests: priests hunted down; betrayed; left lingering in prison; condemned as traitors; executed.

3

MISSIONARY PRIEST

On 29 June 1630, the Feast of St Peter and St Paul, Nicholas Postgate sailed across the sea to participate in what was known as the English Mission: *in messem Anglicanam* (to gather in the 'English harvest'). He went, according to John Knaresborough, 'with great character'.

As he had come to Douai from Yorkshire, and as we know that after his return he spent the rest of his life in Yorkshire, it is probable that he landed, not at Dover as did the majority coming from the Continent, but at Whitby. Others had done this. Bishop Challoner, in *Memoirs of Missionary Priests* tells how in 1591 a certain Hugo Sewel in the company of two secular priests, Edmund Gennings and Alexander Rawlins, landed near Whitby on an open beach on the side of a high cliff, with great danger to their lives. More danger awaited them in the town when in an inn they were questioned by a pursuivant by the name of Ratcliffe. They were fortunate, however, in finding refuge for the time being in the home of a Catholic gentleman two or three miles outside Whitby. Subsequently the priests were executed: Edmund Gennings at Gray's Inn Fields in 1591 and Alexander Rawlins, after four years of missionary work in Yorkshire, on 7 April 1595, outside the city of York in the company of the Jesuit Henry Walpole, a scholar, poet and priest.

By the time Postgate arrived back in England the Abbey at Whitby had long been dissolved. This took place in December 1539. The Parish Church of St Mary had continued in use for a while, then Mass ceased to be celebrated and, in 1570, a Protestant minister was installed. Chapels in the neighbourhood also passed gradually into Protestant hands.

For some twenty years Catholics at Whitby were afforded help by Lady Katherine Scrope, widow of Lord Scrope of Bolton and then of Sir Richard Cholmley. A staunch Catholic, she had lived at the Abbey House close to St Hilda's Abbey, from 1578, with her son Sir Henry Cholmley, a Protestant, and his wife, formerly Margaret Babthorpe, who belonged to a well-known Yorkshire Catholic family. Sir Henry allowed freedom of conscience to the Catholics in his household. According to the *Memoirs* of his son, Sir Hugh Cholmley, the Abbey House provided a 'receptacle' for seminary priests coming from overseas and landing at Whitby. This, however, came to an end in 1598 when, on the death of his mother, Sir Henry moved, probably for financial reasons, to a family house at Roxby near Staithes. But the Abbey House was not the only refuge for priests of Whitby. Bagdale Old Hall is said to have harboured clergy and to have had a 'priest's hole', also an underground passage leading to the quay.

Contacts between the North Riding and English Catholics on the Continent had existed for a considerable time. In 1583 a Scarborough shipmaster was arrested for importing rosaries and vestments. In 1585 a shipment of 500 Catholic catechisms, fifteen Latin New Testaments, and other Catholic reading matter was intercepted. Boys were sent when possible to Flanders, in pairs, for education. In 1562 a son of a Mr Hawksworth of York and Mount St John, Thirsk, shared rooms with a student by the name of Tessimond from York.

The first seminary priests to come to Yorkshire were

under the direction of Cardinal Allen, their faculties being received through him. Once on the sea or across the sea, they were left largely to their own initiative and ingenuity.

In 1585, however, the Cardinal provided them with a leader, John Mush, to whom he delegated quite considerable authority. He was the most renowned secular missionary priest in Yorkshire and the spiritual director of Margaret Clitherow. At one time a servant in the household of the distinguished Dr Vavasour from the East Riding, Mush was an outspoken recusant; having taken himself to Douai in 1576 he was sent on to Rome from where, encouraged by Dr Allen, he returned to England. There he stayed at various rest-centres or 'clearing houses' where priests could break their journeys, have food and rest. One was Grosmont or Grosmont Priory, near Egton. It was probably from here that Thomas Clarke, an apostatized priest, sometime in the period 1592–3 said Mass at Egton (at 'Fatherleys and Postgates') also at a farmhouse at Mulgrave. Upsall Castle, near Thirsk, was another such rest centre, kept by Lady Constable, wife of the owner, the conformist M.P., Sir Henry Constable. Priests were captured there in 1609; below the castle was a maze of vaults that provided means of escape into the countryside. Another place of shelter was the Shambles at York, kept for priests by Margaret Clitherow. It was usual for priests to travel in pairs – passing, for example, as a merchant and his clerk. A companion of John Mush in York was Thomas Bell, a convert Anglican minister who organized the saying of Mass for prisoners in York Castle.

On his return from Douai Nicholas Postgate became chaplain to Lady Hungate at Saxton Hall, ten miles south-west of York, close to where the battle of Towton was fought in the Wars of the Roses. J. C. H. Aveling identifies this Lady Hungate with Jane, daughter of George Middleton from Leighton in the county of Lancaster – the family to which Margaret Clitherow (née Middleton) belonged. Lady Jane was the third wife of Sir William Hungate who died childless in 1634. Postgate stayed on at Saxton until the widow's death which the parish register records as having taken place on 30 May 1642.

The main residence of the Hungates was Huddleston Hall at Sherburn-in-Elmet, but it is clear from the York visitation records that Lady Hungate lived at Saxton Hall. Again J. C. H. Aveling identifies Saxton Hall as the present Manor Farm: a plain, rectangular stone farm-house above the door of which is a coat-of-arms including the arms of Hungate and Saxton. However, G. E. Kirk in his history of Saxton Church (1960) implies that this is a nineteenth-century replacement of the earlier building. He also quotes from the Visitation Book for 1633: 'All the Papists above meet divers times together sometimes at Mr Francis Hungate house & some tymes at Jo: Powells.' Saxton Hall estate later passed into the Gascoigne family when the last heir, Mary Hungate, married Sir Edward Gascoigne of Parlington. There are two Hungate portraits at Lotherton Hall with other Gascoigne ones; these now belong to the Leeds Corporation.

During this period Nicholas Postgate is said to have visited Barnbow Hall which belonged to the Gascoigne family. According to an inventory made in 1661, on the death of Anne, Lady Gascoigne, the house (demolished in 1721–2) had thirty-five rooms, a chapel and vestry and what came to be known as 'Mr Postgate's room'.

About five miles from Tadcaster was Hazlewood Castle, the seat of the Vavasours, one of England's most distinguished Catholic families. Since the year 1972 it has been used as a retreat house and conference centre by the Carmelite Fathers (O. Carms) from Aylesford. Postgate would have heard from Sir Thomas Vavasour how, when the latter was riding with a servant into York on 27 March 1634, he saw, as he passed the Knavesmire, the place of execution, the earth heaving on a recently dug grave. Dismounting, the two men unearthed the still breathing body of Jon Bartendale, a strolling player, who had been hanged for felony. He survived the ordeal, was granted pardon and lived for many years in the service of the Vavasours.

In April 1642, while Nicholas Postgate was still at Saxton, Charles I and the Prince of Wales, later Charles II, were at the Manor House at Bootham Bar when John Lockwood, a priest from Sowerby, near Thirsk, caught in the house of a widow in Thornton-le-Street, was executed at York at the age of eighty-one. On the same occasion Edward Catherick from Carlton, near Richmond, was put to death at York; he had come from Douai in 1635. In 1642 another priest, Edward Wilkes, died in prison in York.

After the death of Lady Hungate, Nicholas Postgate moved to Holderness to the residence of the Dowager Viscountess Dunbar at Halsham, the Dower House of the Burtons of Burton Constable. She used to be known as the 'old lady Dunbar'. Her husband, Sir Henry Constable, who had been created 1st Viscount Dunbar in 1620, had died of wounds at Scarborough in 1645 during the Civil War; he was the son of Thomas Smith of Bridgeholme Green, which meant an association between Nicholas Postgate of Egton Bridge and the Holderness family. The house at Halsham was still used as a Mass centre in the eighteenth century.

In 1659, when Lady Dunbar died, Postgate went to a junior branch of the Constable family at Everingham (North Humberside). At Christmas 1662 he was one of a number of distinguished guests invited back to share in a celebration on the recovery by the family of property lost under the penal laws. Moreover in 1665 Sir Philip Constable left him the sum of £5 'if still alive'. Also in 1672 George Constable, steward of the family, left a pound to his 'good friend Mr Poskett'. On the receipt for this is one of the few autographs of Nicholas Postgate that have come down. Another is in a book of moral casuistry in St Hedda's Church, Egton Bridge.

While at Everingham he served Kilvington Castle and Kilvington Hall, a little north of Thirsk, close to the Hambledon Hills; the property of the Saltmarshe and Meynell families. Thomas Meynell of Kilvington, born in 1564, was imprisoned for four years at Hull, then in York Castle. A Mrs Meynell who visited Postgate when he was in prison in York before his martyrdom was possibly a daughter-in-law of this Thomas.

For the survival of the Catholic Church in England an immense debt is owed to the landed gentry, even if we allow for the fact that, as time went on, an increasing number apostatized under growing pressures – financial, professional and social. As churches and chapels were closed or taken over by Protestants, large houses, mostly in the country, had become, in many instances, the few places where the faithful could assemble secretly to hear Mass and receive the Sacraments.

The owner of the house, meanwhile, was burdened by penal taxation for the crime of being a Catholic; he was debarred, too, from service to the Crown, and fined heavily for refraining to attend a Protestant church. He was also ostracized by non-Catholic neighbours. This, however, was not always so. There were instances where Protestants, far from betraying their Catholic friends and acquaintances, did all they could to alleviate their hardships. And Catholics who had apostatized continued in some instances to make the Mass available for tenants and neighbours, as did Lord Montagu of Cowdray.

Nicholas Postgate, from the time of his return to England from Douai in 1630 lived, until the early 1660s, in the homes of the gentry as a priest, a chaplain to a particular family. But to escape the charge of high treason he was obliged to assume a role, for example as a tutor, secretary, steward or servant.

Precisely which role he had in any given family, we do not know, but this was how things were – the gentry and the priest were dependent one upon the other in their respective ways. The priest provided the Mass, the Sacraments, a spiritual life – this last depending not solely on the priest but on the response of the patron and his family. In return, the patron was responsible for the priest's upkeep and for his safety in so far as this could be maintained.

Sometimes the relationship between priest and family was good. The little we know suggests that in Postgate's case this was so. When Sir William Hungate died at Saxton, Postgate, as we have seen, stayed on with the widow until her death. Again, after he had left the Constable family at Everingham he was invited back. Had there been tension, this would not have been so. Besides, all we know about Postgate suggests a calm, gentle, serene disposition. He did not, we may conclude, come into the category of somewhat uncouth clerics whom Joseph Berington classifies as 'unpleasant in manner'.

If, however, we consider in general terms (not specifically in regard to Postgate) the relationship between priest and patron or protector, this was not always easy. Fundamentally the priest (outside his sacerdotal role which no human power could touch) was in the position of a servant. The patron appointed the priest without permission from or reference to a bishop; equally he could get rid of him. No matter by what name a priest might be called, in relation to his patron he remained, I repeat, a servant. If the patron was arrogant or harsh the position occupied by the priest could be far from enviable. Edwin Burton in *The Life and Times of Bishop Challoner 1691–1781* quotes an instance of a priest standing at the altar, ready to say Mass and waiting for his employer to say: 'Mr . . . you may begin.' Richard Lascelles in his *Little Way How to Hear Mass*, written in 1644, complains of housewives who presumed to teach a priest how to wipe a chalice, and of others who protested if Mass was said too slowly for their taste. According to Sergeant's *Dialogue* of 1667, a priest had usually to be content with shabby quarters. A Protestant maid is recorded as saying that the priest was respectably dressed but slept in a garret!

Indeed sometimes one cannot but recall the atmosphere in Georges Bernanos's *Journal d'un Curé de Campagne* permeating the relationship between M. Le Curé and M. le Comte and Mme. la Comtesse. Moreover, not many years ago in our own country a titled gentleman invited to his house, to discuss some problem, a monsignor staying in the neighbourhood. The butler on opening the door said, with a condescending wave of his hand: 'The servants' entrance, if you please, Your Reverence.'

In Postgate's day the difficulties between clergy and laity, as well as between Secular clergy and Regulars – the Regulars being mainly Jesuits, Benedictines, a few Franciscans and the occasional Dominican – were intensified by the fact that, since the time when Catholic Bishops had been deprived of their sees by Elizabeth in 1559 there was no Catholic Bishop in England (in the sense in which we used the word today) until the restoration of the Hierarchy in 1850. During the eight years from 1623 to 1631 there were two titular Bishops, one following the other: Dr William Bishop who died after nine months in office, followed by Dr Richard Smith who resigned in 1631. Then, despite efforts to appoint as his successor Philip, Cardinal Howard (chaplain to Catherine of Braganza, Queen of Charles II), the vacancy was filled only in the year 1685 by Dr John Leyburn, formerly President of Douai.

These men were Vicars Apostolic, not Bishops in the usual sense of the word, not, that is to say, Bishops in Ordinary. In brief, a Bishop in Ordinary has full jurisdiction over a diocese and is assisted by a Chapter of Canons in accordance with the normal style of Church government. A Vicar Apostolic, on the other hand, is a titular Bishop; he has no diocese or chapter and his powers are restricted. He is the kind of Bishop appointed to a missionary country where government is not yet stabilized; his nominal see is *in partibus infidelium*, in a country that is not Christian – in many instances it may be Moslem. William Bishop was consecrated to the see of Chalcedon. So was Richard Smith. And John Leyburn, to that of Adrumetum.

This paucity of Bishops in penal times, whereby neither clergy nor laity had an effective authority to whom each could turn, presented a variety of problems. One of these was the prolonged disagreement between secular clergy and those who belonged to a religious Order – Jesuits for example. A Secular, for instance in conferring the Sacrament of Penance, derived from the Bishop his authority to give absolution. But what about a Religious, that is, a Regular? Was not the authority of his Superior sufficient? This point occupied the thoughts of many, including Nicholas Postgate. In October 1631, he was one of eleven Yorkshire priests who signed a declaration supporting Richard Smith, Bishop of Chalcedon and Vicar Apostolic of England, in his contention that members of religious Orders needed his approbation before they were entitled to hear confessions.

In 1688 England and Wales were divided into four Vicariates, each ruled by a Vicar Apostolic, who was a titular Bishop. Eventually, in the mid-nineteenth century, by the apostolic letter of Pope Pius IX, *Universalis*

Ecclesiae, dated 29 September 1850, the Hierarchy was restored to England.

During the period 1584 to 1679 (the year in which Nicholas Postgate was executed) no effective diocesan structure existed in England. The missionary priests on their return from Douai or seminaries elsewhere, worked where they could. Often, like Postgate, they worked in their native areas, but others moved from district to district, either in the course of their apostolic labours or to elude those in pursuit of them.

4

THE MOORS

The life of Nicholas Postgate as a priest falls into two parts: the years spent in the homes of the Catholic gentry, followed by those during which he lived on the moors, in poverty and simplicity, going from place to place, seeking out the poor and needy.

Precisely why, when he was now over sixty, he chose to leave the relative security he had enjoyed for years (relative, indeed, for any day a priest could be tracked down, hounded, arrested) we do not know. We can only reflect, surmise.

By this time the Catholic gentry, as a result of increasing fines, restrictions and regulations imposed by the penal laws, were living in ever more stringent circumstances. Resident chaplains, for reasons of economy, were less in demand. Families, too, had apostatized, but not the ones who had sheltered Postgate, nor were they the kind to turn him out; as we have seen, he was on good terms with his patrons.

There are other facts to take into account.

It is significant that, having spent his boyhood at Egton Bridge on the edge of the moors, in later years he returned to the moors. His life has shape. The words of the poet T. S. Eliot apply to Nicholas Postgate: 'In my beginning is my end.' So do these words in reverse: 'In my end is my beginning': the motto of Mary Queen of Scots. In the beginning the moors; at the end the moors.

Kirkdale House was on the fringe of the moors. Redbarns, the house in which Nicholas Postgate was arrested looks on to a splendid expanse of moorland. He is spoken of as the Priest of the Moors, the Martyr of the Moors.

Born of relatively humble stock, possibly he felt an urge deep within him to live a life of greater simplicity, greater austerity, one that would leave him free to devote himself to the care of the poor, and enable him to bring the Mass to the poor. His sympathies were with the poor. He lived, he himself says, as the poor live. He felt for them a concern so compelling that, he whimsically confesses, it fell little short of pride.

A change of direction can come about comparatively late in life. We have only to recall Paul-Emile Léger, a much respected Cardinal-Archbishop of Montreal, who, having played an important role in his own country and in the Second Vatican Council, took himself off to work in a leper colony.

Again, it is not uncommon in later years to experience a hankering, a nostalgia, for the scenes and environment of childhood. The child who had belonged to the moors, now advanced in years, came back to the moors. It was not solely the moors in their wild, wide-flung beauty that summoned him, it was the people scattered over their vast areas – his people: independent, stout-hearted, self-reliant, hardy, but isolated and often in extreme poverty. At the risk of his life he sought them out. That was three hundred years ago. Today I have heard him called 'the Good Samaritan of the Moors'.

Ugthorpe

Sometime in the early 1660s Nicholas Postgate went to live on the moorland near Ugthorpe about nine miles from Whitby.

The site of his small cottage built of rough stone is

occupied today by a farmhouse, visible from the road that crosses the moors between Guisborough and Whitby. It is known as the Hermitage or sometimes as Postgate House. A wall going back to his time is contained in the lowest of three adjoining buildings (making up the one farm) below a chimney on the right as you face the Hermitage. A horizontal line formed by plaster indicates the height of the original walls.

Despite the passage of time, despite reconstructions, 'improvements' and the like, it is not difficult to visualize Postgate's dwelling as once it was. Still, today, you can come across, from time to time on the moors, a small, single-storied building, made of rugged stone, and oak-beams, very old and thatched, its floor of natural earth. Or you can study a book written by Canon Atkinson, Vicar of Danby from 1847 to 1900, telling all you could want to know about ancient, primitive 'cabins and cots', places that offered shelter to man and animals alike. But perhaps most interesting of all, in *A Handbook for Ancient Whitby and its Abbey*, are the descriptions and photographs of primitive cottages in Postgate's native area of Egton.

Some details about the cottage at Ugthorpe have come down in an article, 'Nicholas Postgate, the Old Catholic Priest', published in 1838 and reprinted in Dom Bede Camm's *Forgotten Shrines*. This helps to build up a picture, and is the more valuable because 'the little cell', as the writer calls it, was demolished in 1870. Moreover the fact that it was for so long, we read, a place of pilgrimage, testifies to Postgate's renown as a martyr; his *fama martyrii*. Prefacing the article is an affectionate Dedicatory Epistle, initialled J. W. and addressed to the Catholic Priest at Ugthorpe (Fr Nicholas Rigby), in which the author reveals that he is a convert to Catholicism and has written with the purpose of atoning for having wronged the Church by his former prejudices.

The building, he says, was one of the poorest imaginable, standing, at the time of writing, alone, on the desolate moor where it had stood all those years, a mere 'cattle-shed' to look at, a single chimney indicating that it was a human habitation. Two or three ancient ash trees reached out in its direction their naked, wind-wracked branches as if to draw to it the attention of some passing traveller.

The door, the writer tells us, was low; to enter, you had to bow your head. The thatched roof was low and the narrow latticed windows were deeply inset in the roughly fashioned walls. The floor was paved unevenly. There were two rooms. The smaller was a bedroom. In the other, in which there was a hearth for a peat fire, Nicholas Postgate used to offer a welcome to all who cared to come, especially his scattered moorland 'parishioners'. Many, clinging to their religion the more closely because it was proscribed by those in authority, would come in secret, respecting their pastor the more because he was happy to run the risk of persecution for their sakes. Many, too, were the children who came to see him, to listen to him, to receive his blessing. Or he would offer hospitality to a passing traveller – the occasional priest, on his way, perhaps, from the Continent, riding by after landing at Whitby. All were sure of a welcome. And yet, as he well knew, a knock on the door could be a prelude to arrest, imprisonment, execution.

Outside the building, the writer adds, were flowers in profusion. Postgate was fond of flowers; he felt as did Fernand Portal over two hundred years later: '*La fleur parle de Dieu, le faut mieux connaître.*' He is said to have introduced to Yorkshire, from the Continent, the arum lily and the daffodil. Some like to think that we are indebted to him for the splendid daffodils that to this day grow in their thousands at Farndale. Anyway, in his lifetime he had his little garden there on the moors. After his death pilgrims inspired by misplaced devotion stripped it of all they could lay hands on, greedy to display in their own gardens perennial relics. Only an odd bloom survived their predatory grasp. That Nicholas Postgate should have grown flowers was appropriate. A flower is a symbol of peace. Postgate was a man of peace.

From the cottage the moor reached away north, west and south. Vast, impressive, now sombre, now sunlit. Infinite in variety of colour and shifting light. To the east a strip of cultivated land stretched, like a promontory, towards a distant bay on the surface of which sailing ships, diminished by distance to the size of white-winged birds, skimmed the blue. Eyes, seeking a green oasis, came to rest on the fields, woods and park of Mulgrave, its Castle reaching up from a hump in the valley.

There was nothing forbidding about Nicholas Postgate. A warmth of heart drew others to him. He encouraged the diffident by confiding to them his own shortcomings. 'The humanity of the man', it was said of him, 'overcame the prejudices of the priest' – perhaps 'preconceived ideas' would be better than prejudices. He won over the most unpromising persons, treating the bad as if they were good, those who had injured him as though they had done him a service. This was not naivety. It was an intuitive understanding of human nature in an era when psychology, as we understand it today, was unknown. It was genuine Christianity. 'Return good for evil. Do good to those who despitefully use you.'

He made strangers into friends, friends into Christians. That was three hundred years ago. In our own times a Protestant is quoted in Yorkshire as saying of Nicholas Postgate that he was the most genuine Christian of whom he had ever heard.

'The Priest of the Moors' has a place in *England's Reformation*, a satiric poem in four cantos composed by Thomas Ward who knew Postgate personally. Born at Danby Castle in Eskdale in 1642, Ward, after being brought up a Calvinist, became a Catholic and wrote several works in defence of Catholicism. Having travelled in France and Italy and served for five or six years in the Papal Guard, he returned to England in 1685. He died in France in 1708.

In the fourth canto of his poem Ward treats of the so-called Popish Plot of 1678. After describing evidence 'cooked up' by Titus Oates and his gangsters, and having castigated other informers of the period, he goes on to speak of 'Father Posket', using the word 'Father' – as I have earlier suggested – as a term of respect, verging on endearment, and reiterating what many others had said, that Nicholas Postgate was condemned to death 'not as a plotter but as a priest':

> Nor spar'd they Father Posket's blood,
> A reverend priest, devout and good,
> Whose spotless life in length was spun
> To eighty years, and three times one.

Thomas Ward mentions the thatched cottage, two miles from Mulgrave Castle, buried in winter beneath drifts of snow. It was there, 'the lingy moor' (as he calls it in a marginal note – ling being the species of heather most common in those parts), that God in his providence had established Nicholas Postgate 'For Blackamor's far greater good';

Ward concludes a note in the margin with the brief, moving words: 'I knew him well.'

The Hermit of the Moors

'For Blackamor's far greater good.'

Nicholas Postgate is called sometimes the 'Hermit of the Moors'. 'Hermit'? Yes, the word is acceptable if a distinction is made between a hermit and recluse. A recluse, as the word is generally understood, shuns the company of his fellowmen. A hermit, whether he lives on the moors, in the desert or in a monastery, remains, like his Master, the servant of others.

St Antony the Hermit was also known as the Physician of Egypt. St John of the Cross, a Carmelite belonging to an Order that, according to tradition, goes back to Elijah in the wilderness, was a hermit in temperament; he liked quiet. He liked to sit in silence watching fish darting to and fro in a stream, to look out of the window of his cell at the flowers or at the stars. In Lisbon, when his fellow friars wanted him to go with them to see a nun who professed to have bleeding wounds, he would have none of it; instead, he walked along the bank of the Tagus, reading the Bible. Yet he cared deeply for his brethren: if one of them was depressed, John would take him out on to the thyme-scented sierras; if one was ill he would cook him an appetizing dish and coax him to eat. Equally, Charles de Foucauld, living alone in his hermitage in the depths of the Sahara, devoted himself to the welfare of the Tuareg, putting himself totally at the disposal of these, his brothers, to the extent that he would interrupt his thanksgiving after Mass sooner than keep them waiting. 'He never kept us waiting,' they said of him after his death: it was the highest tribute they could have paid him.

These three are persons who in their different ways resolved what, in his book *Searching for God*, Cardinal Basil Hume, O.S.B., calls 'the tension' between the desert and the market-place, meaning by desert 'withdrawal so as to meet God', and by market-place 'involvement in pastoral situations'. Substitute 'moors' for 'desert' and we have Nicholas Postgate. Nor do the words 'desert' (or 'moors') and 'market-place' imply an either–or; the two can overlap.

In his humble dwelling at Ugthorpe, Postgate shared what he had; he gave counsel and encouragement. When he was going to say Mass he spread sheets on the hedgerow, as if to air them; that was his sign.

The old Mass-House, Egton.

A modern wood carving of Fr Postgate,
carved out of English oak.

Fr Postgate's bone crucifix which he wore at his martyrdom.

The Postgate Cross with Whitby in the background. It is thought that Fr Postgate may have held meetings here.

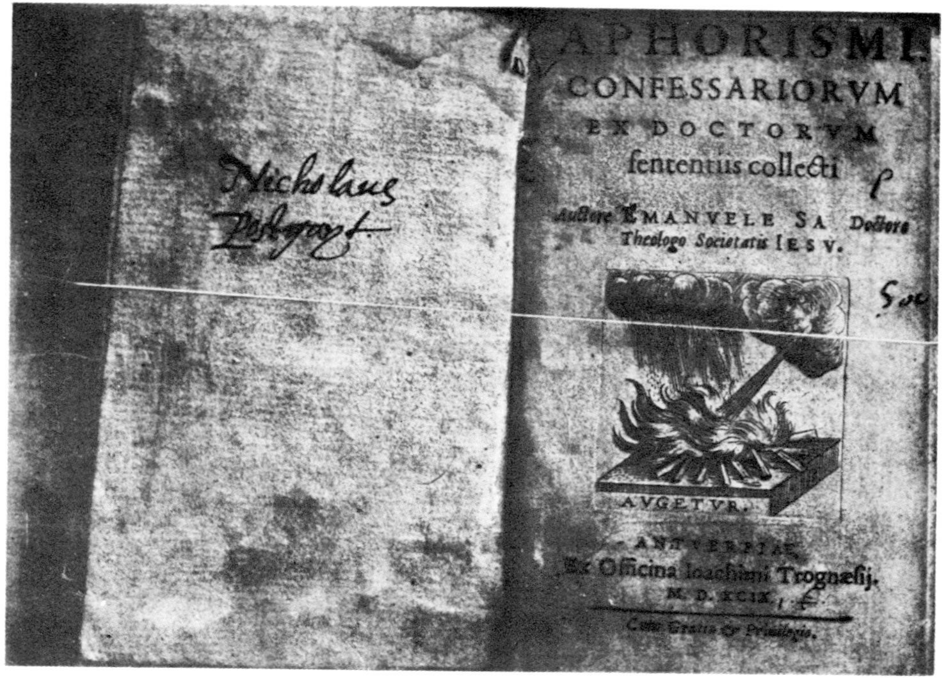

A book with the autograph signature of Fr Postgate.

While he was at Ugthorpe, it is probable that he sometimes said Mass at Ugthorpe Old Hall, home of the Radcliffes who had owned Mulgrave Castle until it was taken from them because they refused to apostatize. 'William Radcliffe of Ugthorpe, gent', is listed among recusants who appeared at the Quarter Sessions in 1641. Writing of Ugthorpe Hall, Dom Bede Camm mentions an outhouse, used as a cow-byre, to the left of the Hall, in which, he says, there was a priest's hiding-place in a chimney. He mentions a second byre on the right where 'people still living' (that was in 1910) remembered their parents recalling the time when Mass was said there. There was, Dom Camm adds, what would have been a holy-water stoup or 'more probably an aumbry'. The Hall, to this day has its priest's hiding place and holy-water stoup or aumbry.

Yes, the moors were Nicholas Postgate's parish. It covered, roughly, an expanse to the north-east, called Cleveland Moor or Blackamoor – extending from the coast, in the Whitby area, north-west to Ugthorpe and on towards Guisborough, then south to Egton, Egton Bridge, Eskdale, Grosmont, and back in the direction of Whitby – taking in Sleights, then south again over the Goathland moors and down to Pickering.

It is reasonable, too, to suppose that he went west to Osmotherley where in about 1665 the Franciscans had opened a house to provide for the pilgrims on their way to the ancient, much loved shrine of Our Lady of Mount Grace; the shrine rested against a wooded slope, its ruins restored by the Eldon and Scrope families. This is apart from places, mentioned earlier, where he had been chaplain to a number of families. Nor is this the moment to speak of Brompton where he was taken after being arrested, nor of York, where he was imprisoned and executed; although even the conditions in York did not prevent him from spreading the Gospel by word and example up to the moment of his death.

Those who today cover long distances by motor vehicles do not always appreciate the amount of ground Nicholas Postgate covered on foot. There is no mention of his riding a horse. Some priests did so; some did not. A horse cost money. The point has been made (rightly or wrongly – see John Bossy's *The English Catholic Community*) that riding a horse became associated with a growing trend towards a gradually more 'gentlemanly' standard of life for the clergy.

The extent of Nicholas Postgate's pastoral work and his manner of life is attested by the Latin translation of a letter he wrote in English in 1664 (the English version is not extant) reporting his activities in Yorkshire. It was written to Dr George Leyburn, President of the English College at Douai from 1652 until he resigned in 1670, who had it translated into Latin to be incorporated into a memorandum submitted to Rome, to the Sacred Congregation of *de Propaganda Fide*, concerning the work done by the *alumni* of Douai who were mission priests in England.

He had been on the Mission (in his instance, in Yorkshire) for thirty-four years, he says, and he goes on to give some details of his ministry. He had joined in marriage 226 couples, baptized 593 infants, buried 719 dead, and brought 2,400 persons into the Church. At the time of writing, he adds, he had in all 600 penitents and could have had more. He did not ask for respite; he was in the world to work, he told himself again and again. '*Identidem repeto. Cur requiem quaeris, cum natus sis ad laborem?*' ('Why do you seek rest when you were born for hard work?')

No Lack of Good Will

It was not good will he lacked, but helpers: '*Voluntas quidem haud mihi deest, deest tamen adjutor.*'

He would have appreciated more fellow-priests, but

he was in touch with those there were – some of them from Douai. Towards the end of his ministry he had the help of a Mr Thomas Goodrick, born in the North Riding, educated at Douai, returned to Yorkshire in 1631, and last heard of in 1669. Another was John Jowsie, a native of Guisborough; he too was educated at Douai and was in Yorkshire in 1648. His will was proved on 4 June 1678.

Other Priests

Other priests Postgate knew included Thomas Faceby of sturdy recusant stock who lived with the Meynells at North Dalton, Matthew Berry who worked mostly in Cleveland, and Francis Hodgson who was at first with the Withams at Cliffe, later at Biggin House. There was also Marmaduke Dalton, a convert distinguished for his writing and intellectual pursuits – supported by an annuity of £40 from his father. Also working in the Egton district in Postgate's time was George Smith, an Augustinian – he, too, received an annual stipend, from his family, of £12, and probably lived at Bridgeholme Green, formerly the manor house, where the door, it was said, was open day and night so that a priest could find food and hospitality. John Marsh, esteemed for his wit and ability, after being hunted by the spy Thomas Dangerfield and having taken refuge in Lancashire, came back to Egton where, it is said, he kept house for himself, probably at Bridgeholme. In 1693 he succeeded to Nicholas Postgate's area, devoting himself, it is recorded, 'to this most laborious place', to 'a great multitude of poor living on the moors'. Egton district, it was said, had in 1690 the largest number of recusants in the North Riding.

Postgate used to have contact with the Yorkshire Brethren, a society founded for the relief of infirm priests.

At the first General Assembly held at Bootham Bar, York, on 29 August 1672, he had voted by proxy through Christopher Bankes, the Vicar General. He attended the second Assembly on 22 November 1676 at Peaseholme Green. There is no exact record of the attendance at the third meeting held at Mr Hunter's, Petergate, York, but twenty-two or twenty-three priests were present. There was a hint of chaos: the 'fearful noise of ye pretended popish plot . . . all confusion!'

Nicholas Postgate met his death in time to escape the attentions of Ursula Hawkswell, of the Ugthorpe region, who, having become a Protestant, made a habit of denouncing Catholic priests. She saw to it that John Danby was imprisoned in York in 1708. A tombstone in the churchyard at Loftus bears the words: 'Mr John Danby, Priest of the Church of Rome 1719.' Another victim of the indomitable Ursula was the unfortunate George Bostock, a cleric who lived at Bridgeholme Green and went around as a gardener. He was working in the garden of the Smith family at Bridgeholme when, as the result of being kept standing in the cold while answering the questions of pursuivants, he caught a chill and died.

During this time Bishop Thomas Dominic Williams, O.P., was made Vicar Apostolic of the Northern Region. The news that a Dominican – and a Welshman at that – was being appointed caused consternation; the long-standing bad feeling between secular clergy and Regulars had not died down. At first no one would offer him a roof over his head. Eventually the Yorkshire Brethren, with characteristic generosity, granted him goods to the value of twenty-two guineas and the sum of £20 annually.

The late Fr David Quinlan, who devoted the greater part of his ministry to researching into the lives of Nicholas Postgate and his successors, was looking one day into a hiding-hole on the moors where, in the eighteenth century, two priests, Luke Potts and Monox Hervey, had taken refuge after being suspected of what was regarded as their excessive enthusiasm for Jacobites. Suddenly Fr Quinlan heard a voice asking what he was up to. Having explained that he had been reading about these priests in Monox Hervey's diary, he heard his questioner comment dourly: 'Us knows history for it gets into t'books . . .'

Monox Hervey could be no less dour. After recounting his adventures on the moors on a night in winter, followed by imprisonment in York, he concludes, good Yorkshireman though he was, with the prayer:

> From the moors in Yorkshire
> Good Lord deliver us. Amen.

To Monox Hervey we are indebted for the reconciliation to the Church of the tiresome Ursula Hawkswell, on 15 December 1734. There she stood in the church at Ugthorpe, on the Third Sunday in Advent, a lighted candle in her hand, the congregation crying for joy at her change of heart, she for sorrow at the thought of the sins she had committed, the scandals she had caused.

5

THE APOSTOLATE OF THE MOORS

Tramping the Moors

Nicholas Postgate visited his people in season and out, baptizing, bringing Holy Communion, comforting the dying. Sometimes he said Mass in their homes. This was a link with the early Church when, as we know from the New Testament, Mass was often said in private houses – a link, too, with the 'house Masses' as we know them today.

Postgate entered fully into the lives of his people. As recusants they were in danger. So was he. His was the greater, in that the fact of his being a priest was itself a criminal offence, putting his life at stake. He visited them stealthily, moving from one place of refuge to another, aware that there could be a pursuivant on his track.

The Priest of the Moors, he tramped the moors wearing 'all thirty years' a brown tunic resembling a monk's habit, and over it, to protect him from the rain, a white cape made of canvas. He is said to have had a short beard as a protection against a recurrent throat infection. In an ancient picture painted on a wooden panel, said to be of Postgate and now in Whitby Museum, his white beard is full length, his hair white, his complexion pale, his eyes a light blue, and his expression gentle. In the picture, he wears over the brown tunic not a cape but, flung across his left shoulder like the fold of a toga, a length of material that is a deeper blue than his eyes. He carries a staff in his left hand. Apart from the pleasant colouring, it is not a satisfactory picture. A somewhat blank expression fails to convey his character, his intelligence and humour. I prefer the rugged wooden statue carved in our own day by Mr Tom Whitaker of Littlebeck.

Faithful to his priestly calling, Postgate tramped the moors in all seasons, all weather, and at all hours. He crossed them in the glimmering dawn, in broad daylight, in the milky pallor of the moon, under austere glinting stars, in driving rain, and in whirling snow. He saw the moors illuminated by shafts of light breaking from a glowering sky shrouded in mist, shadowed by floating clouds, reaching away to the dreamy blue of distant hills merging into oncoming dusk.

He saw burial mounds rounded like puddings, scarps jutting against the sky, the brilliant yellow of furze, from time to time a glimpse of the sea, raindrops quivering on the fronds of bracken, black-faced sheep cropping sparse grass.

He heard the bleat of lambs and their mothers' deeper, reassuring bleat; the soaring, throbbing note of a lark, the crying of gulls. He felt the breath-taking force of the moorland wind, the Yorkshire wind which (John Ruskin reminds us) is like none other, in that it is so strong you can lean against it without falling, as against 'a quickset hedge'.

He was familiar with roughly hewn stone crosses set here and there to guide travellers on their way, and bid them too, as a fifteenth-century document tells us, to 'think on Hym that dyed on the Cross, and worship Hym above all things'.

Where else were his thoughts, what else was his objective when, regardless of personal safety, he made welcome all who approached his lonely moorland dwelling? – when he spent his last hours in prison in York comforting the afflicted, forgiving those who had done him wrong? Yes, the largeness of his heart, the depth of his spirituality (the two are inseparable) matched the vast expanse of his beloved moors. Did his thoughts echo the joyous cry of the sixth-century Bishop Venantius – Saint Fortunatus – a cry that will echo into eternity?

Faithful Cross, above all other,
One and only noble tree!
None in foliage, none in blossom,
None in fruit thy peer may be;
Sweetest wood and sweetest iron,
Sweetest weight is hung on thee!

In Perspective

It is fitting, if we are to see things in perspective, to recall that Nicholas Postgate, before serving as a chaplain in the relatively sophisticated homes of the gentry, and before devoting himself to his moorland parishioners, spent six years at Douai College. There he studied Scripture, philosophy and theology, presented not solely for their own sake but to foster an orderly, totally orthodox spirituality that would equip him to live day by day and also to face any emergency that might threaten his faith or weaken his courage.

If the words 'religious vocation' have any meaning, there was surely a spark already present in the beginning. To concede this, does not invalidate the fact, as I see it, that in the environment of the moors, his spirituality assumed a new dimension and a brilliance – a vision which, supported by early training and experience, empowered him to endure even martyrdom.

I heard it said of Nicholas Postgate that, no matter what one reads about him or hears about him, his personality remains 'elusive.' The word 'elusive' took me aback. Then, on reflection, I began to understand, for the speaker, who is particularly competent to judge, went on: 'Like John the Baptist, I believe, he would have chosen this to be so – to *decrease* that Another might *increase*.'

It is good to think about Nicholas Postgate along with John the Baptist – along with others, too, who have trodden the path before him and most of all, perhaps, those saintly Northern men and women who down the centuries, in times good and bad, have kept the Faith alive: Hilda the royal Abbess of Whitby; Caedmon, cowherd and poet; Wilfred, monk and bishop; Edwin, Paulinus, Aidan, Cuthbert; and the long line of Benedictines whose abbeys remain beautiful even in their ruins. Yes, let us think of Nicholas Postgate among those who have gone before, and as ready, too, to take his place with others yet to come.

Egton and Egton Bridge

Some four miles south from Ugthorpe you come to the Old Mass House at Egton, where Postgate began to say Mass sometime about 1665.

By 1867 the building was so dilapidated that the owners wanted to pull it down, but were prevailed upon by Canon Callebert, the parish priest, to have it repaired. During the renovations a stone tablet bearing the words *Ye Mass House 1650* was inserted on the outside of the south wall indicating the position inside, in the loft, where in Postgate's time the Tabernacle would have been.

In 1928, while further repairs were being carried out, the walls collapsed and the Mass House had to be rebuilt. The new building incorporates features of the original one, including stones used in the south wall. The staircase was made out of wood taken from the former house. Some of the remaining wood was washed away in the floods of 1930.

While Dom Bede Camm was visiting Egton in the year 1908, a Mr Buchanan of Whitby asked Robert Harrison, who lived at Grosmont, if he would draw a plan and elevation of the Mass House. It is reproduced in Dom Bede Camm's *Forgotten Shrines*.

In 1964 George Harrison, who, like his uncle Robert Harrison, lived at Grosmont, constructed with the aid of photographs and plans and such information as he could acquire, a half-inch scale model of the building as he believed it to have been in Postgate's time. He gave this to the Postgate Centre at Egton Bridge, where it can be seen today.

The model represents a simple, one-storied cottage with a thatched roof. On the east side (the back, that is, of the original building) is a small extension at right angles to the cottage. The oratory (that is the loft under the roof) measures fifteen feet by ten and is five and a half feet high. There is no window, only a kind of tunnel through the thatch. The purpose of the tunnel was to let in light – the only light other than the glimmer from the candles on the altar. A tunnel of this kind can be seen in the thatched Spout House, Bilsdale, and another in the Folk Museum at Hutton-le-Hole.

The steeply pitched roof of the Mass House enabled a man of normal height to stand at the centre of the altar. Possibly two or three persons might have knelt; the rest of the congregation would have been in the room below, or standing on the steps leading to the loft. According to a statement signed by Canon Callebert on 19 June 1872, there was a trap-door that, presumably, would have provided an escape route.

Relics

Among the relics associated with Nicholas Postgate in the Lady Chapel in St Hedda's Church, Egton Bridge, several are from the Mass house.

There is the altar-stone, inset in St Hedda's altar of Our Lady. Like many altar-stones of penal times, which to avoid arousing suspicion tended to be simple and unobtrusive, it is a small square of slate. On the surface are scratched five small crosses; there is no receptacle for relics. There is, too, the tabernacle door. On it is represented, in metal, Christ on the Cross and, standing on either side, the Blessed Virgin and St John; a scroll bears the letters I.N.R.I and has the sun at one end, the moon at the other. The actual tabernacle would have been no more than a hole in the wall.

Also from the Mass House is Postgate's chair, its arms and straight back made of wood, its seat woven from rope and worn into holes. Fr Charles Toner, the parish priest of St Hedda's, tells me that he met an elderly non-Catholic lady in the district who told him this chair had been 'cherished' in her family for a generation before being given to a Mr Turnbull of Whitby. This is characteristic of the devotion shown to Nicholas Postgate by others besides Catholics.

There are also from the Mass House two altar candles, – or rather stumps an inch or so high, and an attractive tiger-ware dish, cracked but carefully repaired – possibly used for taking the collection. In 1928, when the roof of the Mass House was being repaired, silver coins (twenty florins and six shillings dating back to the Carolingian and Elizabethan eras) came showering out of the thatch.

Some four years ago they were stolen from St Hedda's Church.

Other relics at St Hedda's are two pyx bags, used for taking the Blessed Sacrament to the sick – both are faded and the worse for wear. One, made of blue and white brocade, its border hung with yellow tassels, was formerly in the possession of Jane Harris, a woman who 'did' for Postgate. The other, of green silk lined with red, was given to Canon Callebert by Ann Readman, an old woman at Egton who belonged to a well-known Catholic family, the Hodgsons of Bigginhouse.

There is also a small crucifix, made of crystal and decorated with silver filigree, containing a relic of the True Cross. Another crucifix is attached to Nicholas Postgate's rosary; the large cream-coloured beads strung close together – one is missing in the third decade – appear to be made of bone. Attached to the rosary is a ball, or boss, made of leather, or possibly, Dom Bede Camm suggests, it is some kind of 'oriental bean' from which hangs a red silk tassel.

Then there is a little book, written in Latin, on moral theology, *Aphorisimi Confessariorum* by the Jesuit Emanuel Sa, dated 1599 and produced by an Antwerp press. Opposite the title page is the owner's signature.

Another relic is a little wooden box inscribed: *TIME DEUM. 1585.* It is about four inches by three by two, and was probably used for carrying Hosts for the Mass. Up to the present it has proved impossible to open.

There is, too, a scrap of brown material, possibly from Postgate's tunic, and a piece of canvas with a button and a button-hole. Among the objects from the Mass House is a door-handle, or hasp, made of iron and deeply pitted. Fr Toner confesses that he finds it hard to understand precisely how it functioned.

A lock of silky white hair is enclosed in a silver reliquary. Similar locks of hair are in the Bar Convent at York and in St Mary's College, Oscott.

In St Annes's Church, Ugthorpe, are two chalices of which one, if not both, was used by Nicholas Postgate. They are mentioned by T. E. Fallow F.S.A. in an article entitled 'Yorkshire Plate and Goldsmiths', published in the *Archaeological Journal* (vol. lxl, no. 241). Mr Fallow thinks the larger is English, and he dates it at about 1630. Engraved on it under a crucifix are the words *Ora pro D.M.F.*, possibly the initials of the wife of Charles Fairfax of York, a close friend of Nicholas Postgate, who, with another woman, a Mrs Meynell of Kilvington, visited the martyr on the day of his execution. The other chalice, the smaller one, which unscrews into three sections and for that reason was particularly convenient for travelling, is French in origin. The cup was decorated with wave-like flames and is Gothic, according to Mr Fallow. It resembles one in the Museum of St Mary's College, Oscott, known as the 'Persecution Chalice'.

There are, in different places, other Postgate relics of a kind that edify some and are distasteful to others. Among these is a fragment of flesh in a glass tube in St Mary's Abbey at Colwich, Staffordshire; a piece of bone at Stonyhurst College, Lancashire; scraps of material stained with blood at Downside Abbey, Bath; bits of the rope with which he was hanged, at the Barr Convent, York, and at Oscott. Somewhere, I am told, there is a vertebra of his spine and the entire lower jaw.

At Ampleforth is a little crucifix made of bone, strangely beautiful, strangely moving, in its stark primitive simplicity. Nicholas Postgate was wearing it when he went to his death.

Then there are the two withered hands, attributed to Nicholas Postgate, each one not unlike a crumpled, discarded glove. To desecrate the hand that had held the body of Christ was not unusual.

One of the hands, apparently the right, is at St Cuthbert's, Old Elvet, Durham, in the care of Fr Tweedy.

The other, at Ampleforth Abbey, was assumed, at least until comparatively recently, to be a left hand. Then a strange thing happened. At a rally held at Ugthorpe on a day of pouring rain in 1974, the two hands, having been laid side by side, were thereupon seen to be each a right hand!

As to the hand at Ampleforth it is wrapped in an L-shaped piece of cloth, probably linen, with a fairly open weave. In the memory of the present Father Abbot and others whom he consulted the relic has long been wrapped in this cloth.

At one time, however, the relic was contained in a parchment instead, which was subsequently lost. A list made in 1934 or thereabouts mentions that the parchment was missing. For further interest it is well worthwhile reading the *Ampleforth Journal* Autumn 1974 (vol. lxxix, III, p. 105), also the letter written by Fr. Alberic Stacpoole, O.S.B. (18.1.78).

Pickering

Pickering has associations with Nicholas Postgate.

To go there from Egton Bridge, strike south across Blackamoor leaving behind, to the right on Egton High Moor, the ancient burial mounds known as the Three Howes. Then on, until you are confronted, near Stape, by Mauley Cross, named after the de Mauleys of Musgrave Castle. It stands up, lonely and rugged, from the wind-swept grass, against a backcloth of larches.

Or you can make a detour to the east, along the River Esk to Grosmont, among its bracken and its silvery boulders, then on to Goathland, a village exposed to every wind, resting upon the open moor yet in reach of woods and waterfalls. Then, from Goathland south-east to the Fylingdales Moor, to Lilla Cross, which dates from the seventh century and is perhaps the oldest Christian monument in the North. The River Esk, Grosmont, Goathland, Mauley Cross, Fylingdales Moor, Lilla Cross – with these Nicholas Postgate would have been familiar. But what about the three giant 'ping-pong balls' or, if you prefer, three balloons anchored to the moorland, manning the Ballistic Missile Early Warning Station? How would he have reacted to these? With the same, quiet, philosophical humour, I fancy, with which he viewed much else.

It is splendid country, devastatingly beautiful, awesome, elemental: open sky, sunshine, racing clouds; sharp, clear air; the crying of birds; the soughing of wind; heath and bell-heather, their purple mingling with the deep-brown of peat and the green of rushes; bilberries and crowberries; hair-grass and cotton-grass; grey, solitary farmsteads; gullies, hillocks and hollows, and, always, the sheep.

South. And still south, verging a little to the west you skirt the Hole of Horcum – frightening in its depth, its vast hollow lined with flame-red bracken, tilled fields and a couple of farms. Such was the route the pursuivants used to follow – their headquarters being at Pickering and Guisborough, each twenty-one miles from Whitby. Approaching riders were easily spotted and Postgate warned.

At some point to the south there is an ancient milestone, the spelling phonetic: PICKRING. A glorious route indeed, but its beauty can carry a threat; looming clouds, enveloping mist, shrilling wind.

Spell it as you will, Pickering is an old market-town and has the ruins of a castle. Two streets lead steeply to the parish church, its walls painted with frescos to teach the truths of Christianity in an age when few in the congregation could read. Pretending to be a gardener, Nicholas Postgate made his way here from Ugthorpe, a hoe in his hand. But he had more than a hoe; he had what nearer our own times came to be spoken of as a priest's 'Mass kit' – the essentials, that is, if he is to consecrate the bread and the wine, and distribute the Hosts.

At Pickering, Postgate stayed in a small thatched cottage in which a gardener had previously lived. It was in a place still called the Martyr's Field, a delightful setting a little way outside the town on the Whitby side, in the shadow of the now ruined castle. Here, as elsewhere, sheets were spread on the hedgerows as a sign that Mass was to be said.

Long after he had been put to death the townspeople continued to be proud of Nicholas Postgate. They would point out a pear tree that he had pruned, and tell how he had visited Charles I when the King was imprisoned in the Castle for a brief spell in 1649. He was remembered, too, as the last priest to say Mass in Pickering before Catholicism was temporarily suppressed in that area by the enforcement of the penal laws.

As he used to tramp the moors to Pickering, he did not know that the day would come when he would go not to Pickering but to Brompton, nearby in the Vale of Pickering on the road to Scarborough – a prisoner in his old age, at the mercy of others, like Peter the Apostle: 'When you were young you girded yourself and went where you chose. In your old age you will stretch forth your hands and another will gird you and take you where you have no wish to go.'

6

THE BEGINNING OF THE END

As to the arrest of Nicholas Postgate there are slight variations in detail. According to the tradition handed down at Egton Bridge, he said Mass on 7 December 1679 in the Mass House at Egton and from there went to baptize the child of a certain Catholic, Matthew Lyth, at a house called Redbarns which stands on the moorland road between Ugglebarnby and Littlebeck, about five miles from Whitby. To this day Mass is said at Redbarns on some special occasions, in what is called 'Father Postgate's room'.

Unwittingly he had set out on what was to be his final journey, one that would lead him from apparent defeat to triumph – to what John Warner, S.J., scholar, historian of the Oates Plot, Provincial (1679–83) of the English Jesuit Province, calls the 'glorious victory of Nicholas Postgate, a priest of the secular clergy at York' (*gloriosa victoria Nicholai Postgate sacerdotis a clero seculo Eboraci*), a passing from the tribulations of time into the joy of eternity. John Warner had reason to be interested in Nicholas Postgate. He himself had studied at the English College at Douai and taught philosophy and theology there for some five years before entering the Society of Jesus. Moreover Nicholas Postgate, as John Warner well knew, was the uncle of Ralph Postgate, S.J., who, having studied at Douai and Rome, became, it will be recalled, twice Rector of the Venerable College, Rome, where he died in 1718.

Nicholas Postgate, under the Act passed in 1585 (27 Elizabeth 1.2) came into the category of 'Jesuits, seminary Priests and such like disobedient persons' and was consequently subject to the death penalty. Nevertheless, because the penal laws had not been at all times rigorously enforced and persecution had tended to come in waves rather than continuously, he had hitherto managed to live an unobtrusive life, devoting himself secretly to his people.

Probably this would have gone on had it not been for the Titus Oates Plot (or Popish Plot): a conspiracy of Catholics, it was alleged, to assassinate King Charles II and restore Catholicism to England, discovered (so Titus Oates, Israel Tonge and others of their kind had claimed) in the year 1678. The allegation came from persons found guilty of perjury, particularly Oates himself, a dishonourable, disreputable, despicable creature, a turncoat, guided by self-interest, who changed his allegiance and his religion (now a Protestant, now a Catholic, now a Protestant) as the fad took him. Mr E. I. Watkin in his book *Roman Catholicism in England from the Reformation to 1950*, points out that accusations from such a man were as ill-founded as those of the Emperor Nero when he accused the Christians of having set fire to Rome.

Nicholas Postgate was in Matthew Lyth's house, where he had come to baptize Lyth's child, when two men arrived to search for arms and ammunition which they suspected, they said, were hidden there for use in the Oates Plot. These were John Reeves and Henry Cockerill, a mariner from Whitby. Also in the house were two Catholic yeomen, Readman and Roe.

Reeves was from Whitby. He is described as an 'exciseman', a 'surveyor', and a 'gauger'. In the context a surveyor means an official who supervised the collecting of taxes. A gauger collected excise duties (duties, that is, levied on home products as distinct from imports), and was so called because he gauged or calculated, for excise purposes, the capacity of casks, vessels and such like.

How Reeves came to be at Whitby is not known. Formerly he had been in London as a personal servant to Sir Edmund Berry Godfrey (1621–78) a much respected Protestant Justice of the Peace at Westminster, to whom Titus Oates, in September 1678, made his first depositions concerning what later came to be known as the Popish Plot. Then on 17 October the same year, Godfrey was found massacred, pierced by his own sword (murder or suicide?) at the foot of Primrose Hill, North London. Because he was a zealous Protestant, Catholics were suspected – two were hanged for the crime at Tyburn on 21 February 1679. This may have contributed to the fact that Reeves abhorred Catholics. John Danby, a Yorkshire priest, in a letter written on 17 February 1709 to John Knaresborough, to whom we are indebted for many details concerning Nicholas Postgate, describes Reeves as 'an implacable enemy of Catholicks as the supposed murtherers of his master'. Incidentally in the same letter Danby encloses for Knaresborough a register that had belonged to Postgate (probably baptisms and the like) and mentions someone who kept 'holy' the day of Postgate's martyrdom – a testimony to the latter's *fama martyrii*.

Reeves certainly made no attempt to conceal his ill-feeling towards Matthew Lyth. He had heard Lyth, he told people, let fall at a wedding the sinister words: 'You talk of Papists and Protestants, but when the roast is ready, I know who will have the first cut.' And he had heard from his companion, William Cockerill, who belonged to the Constabulary at Eskdaleside (that is to say, he was a conservator or keeper of the peace), of other strange words spoken by Lyth in William

Cockerill's house: 'A sorrowful Christmas, a bloody Fastness [Shrove Tuesday], a joyful Easter.' In short, Matthew Lyth was, according to Reeves, a suspicious character, a papist malcontent up to no good. Reeves would seek out the wretch, and see if 'some armes and ammunition' were not to be found in his house.

And so the two men, Reeves and Henry Cockerill, overruling Lyth's resistance and his attempt to conceal Postgate, searched the house. They found neither arms nor ammunition, but they did find 'popish books, relicks and wafers, and severall other things'. They found, too, a 'supposed priest' – Nicholas Postgate. The latter, when asked if the various objects were his, admitted that they were. Asked what he did with them, he said he disposed of them among 'severall persons who desired them for help in their infirmities'. He had been given them, he said, by a Mr Thomas Goodrick and a Mr John Jowsie. They were both priests from Douai who had worked with him, but who were now dead.

Postgate, having been asked his name, gave it as Watson, the name of his grandmother on his father's side; his father, James, had been the son of William Postgate of Kirkdale, who had married a Watson. In appearance, Nicholas said, he resembled that side of the family.

Nicholas Postgate's cause was considered at Westminster in the period 1923 to 1926. When the evidence was examined in Rome in 1929, the Promoter General of the Faith (the Devil's Advocate) praised the courageous, joyous spirit with which the prisoner had faced death. He went on, however, to say he noticed that, when being arrested, Postgate had shown some hesitation: *Non latet me istum . . . aliquam haesitationem ostendisse.* He had in mind, presumably, Postgate's replies about the books, the wafers, and so on, and the fact that he did not at once say he was a priest: 'Let them prove it!' he had said to his questioners. He was entitled to say so; the accused is innocent until proved guilty. No doubt, too, he had to consider the welfare of persons who had harboured him or shown willingness to do so.

Let Them Prove It

'Let them prove it!' The words have a challenging ring. Like many another of the martyrs, Nicholas Postgate was a normal man to whom life was dear. He was deeply human, as was Thomas More. 'A fainter heart than thy frail father thou canst not have,' More said to his daughter. Postgate was not consumed, any more than More had been, with a fanatical craving for death. Yet, if called upon to die he would do so with a light heart, courageously, joyfully, welcoming the moment as God-given, even as he had welcomed each moment of life. This, despite the fear, the agony of mind to which, at such a time, any person of sensitivity is subject, as was Christ himself in Gethsemane.

'Let them prove it!' There is a subtle humour in the words, a shrug of the shoulder. If he is a priest, if he has merited the death penalty, it is for them, not for him, to prove it! The question is flung back at the questioner.

There is the merest touch of irony. The words recall an interchange in the Gospel: 'And Pilate asked him: "Are you the King of the Jews?" And he answered: "You say so".'

Arrested at Redbarns, Postgate was taken the twenty miles across the moors south to Brompton, a town on the road that runs east of Pickering in the direction of Scarborough. Readman and Roe, the yeomen, were also taken.

He who, time and again had crossed the moors at will, crossed them now at the mercy of others set upon his ruin. He was robbed of his freedom. Or so it seemed. But his was a freedom no man could take from him.

At Brompton he was put in the lock-up. The next day Sir William Cayley, the local Justice of the Peace, in the presence of his son, also William Cayley, took statements or depositions from Nicholas Postgate, John Reeves and William Cockerill, also from Robert Langdaile, who, like William Cockerill, was a member of the Constabulary, and from Henry Cockerill, the mariner. In the margin of Postgate's deposition are two large scrawled initials N.P. written by his own hand.

The account given above of Postgate's arrest is compiled from statements made in his own deposition and in that of Reeves. Moreover, William Cockerill said he had often seen 'the person now apprehended', known by the name of Postgate, going about the country; that he was generally believed to be, and was spoken of as, a popish priest. Robert Langdaile added that he had heard of 'the prisoner Posket' and that for many years he had been 'generally accounted a Popish priest'.

From Brompton, Postgate was taken to York, probably by way of Malton, where he was imprisoned in the Castle. Before he left Brompton, other witnesses were examined between 6 March and 11 March. They included Elizabeth Baxter, a spinster about thirty years old, who alone mentioned that by now Postgate was imprisoned in York. Also examined were Elizabeth Wood, wife of Ralph Wood, and Richard Morrice, a tailor from Whitby.

Elizabeth Baxter had often, she said, seen the 'reputed Popish priest' and heard him say Mass several times at Biggin House, the home of John Hodgson, near Ugthorpe. He had given Holy Communion to herself and others about eight or nine years ago. After this she had become a Protestant and attended Protestant services. She lived near Scarborough.

Elizabeth Wood, wife of Ralph Wood, a mariner at

Whitby, had known Postgate for ten or twelve years and had heard him say Mass at Thomas Pattison's house in the Constabulary of Ugthorpe and in Timothy Lyth's house near Gromond Bridge (that is Grosmont). She had received the Sacrament from his hands some seven or eight years ago and seen others do the same. She had been a Protestant for the past six years.

Richard Morrice knew 'Mr. Poskitt, a popish priest'; he had been married by him, had 'received the Sacrament from him after the Popish manner' several times, had seen him give the Sacrament to others and had heard him celebrate Mass. Morrice himself had become a Protestant about twelve years earlier and went 'constantly' to church. Greatly disliked, he was known as the 'Hang Priest'.

In the following year, 1679, among orders made at the Quarter Sessions held at Thirsk in the North Riding on 29 April, was one for the payment of £3 by the Riding Treasurer to John Reeves for 'prosecuting Nicholas Postgate, a Popish priest by him apprehended . . . and upon his [Reeve's] prosecution found guilty of being a Popish priest'.

Later an order was made for the payment to Reeves of £20 for 'apprehending' Nicholas Postgate. It is improbable that he received this. It is said that after prolonged suffering of 'body and mind' Reeves was found drowned. All that is known points to his being mentally unstable. His body was recovered from the Devil's Dump, a deep, sinister pool formed from the water of the Little Beck where it flows past Ugglebarnby to join the Esk at Sleights. Since that time, the saying goes, no fish have been caught in this water. Canon Callebert tested this for himself. But what is not clear is whether there were any beforehand.

7

THE CLIMAX

Prison in York

Of the Castle in York in which Nicholas Postgate was confined only the Clifford Tower remains, around which there used to be a high wall. The prison area was to the south of the Tower; it is now occupied by the Assize Courthouse and the Museum.

Also confined were Matthew Lyth and the yeomen Readman and Roe. Lyth, who declined to say anything that might incriminate Postgate, was detained until after the priest's execution. Readman and Roe managed to secure their release, pleading that they had to bring in the harvest. Some say that Readman made a statement derogatory to Postgate, whereas Roe refused.

Postgate was detained from December 1678 until March 1679. It is probable that it was during the winter months that he composed what has come to be known as the Postgate Hymn, sung to this day in his part of Yorkshire. I heard it sung in a field at Egton Bridge, within a few yards of his birthplace, on 15 July 1979, during the Postgate Rally which was part of the tercentenary celebrations commemorating his death. Again in 1979, it was sung in York on 7 August, the anniversary of his execution; also at Hazlewood Castle.

As well as on other occasions the hymn is sung at the burial of any member of the Ancient Guild of St Joseph and St Hedda – two lines at a time as the body is being carried out of the house, then, as the procession moves to the church or the graveside, all join in:

O Gracious God, O Saviour Sweet,
  O Jesus, think of me.
And suffer me to kiss Thy feet,
  Though late I come to Thee.

Behold, dear Lord, I come to Thee
  With sorrow and with shame,
For when Thy bitter wounds I see
  I know I caused the same.

O Sweetest Lord, lend me the wings
  Of faith and perfect love,
That I may fly from earthly things
  And mount to Thee above.

For there is joy both true and fast
  And no cause to lament.
But here is toil both first and last,
  And cause oft to repent.

But now my soul doth hate the things
  In which she took delight,
And unto Thee, O King of Kings,
  Would fly with all her might.

But oh, the weight of flesh and blood,
  Doth sore my soul detain:
Unless Thy grace doth work, O God,
  I rise but fall again.

And thus, O Lord, I fly about,
  In weak and weary case.
And, like the dove Noe sent out,
  I find no resting place.

My weary wing, Sweet Jesus, mark,
  And when thou thinkest best,

Stretch forth Thy Hand out of the ark
And take me to Thy rest.

For the people of the North Yorkshire Moors, the Postgate Hymn is a special feature in their living relationship with the martyr. It is, as it were, a signature tune, echoing that deep Christocentric faith which is the essence of true Christian living. Still, today, in the Postgate country no other hymn is sung more frequently.

It does not really profit us to know whether Nicholas Postgate composed it after his condemnation or long before. The important thing is that it conveys the entire spirit of the martyr in a timeless context, whether it be the Knavesmire at York three centuries ago or Auschwitz in our own day.

Thomas Ward's poem about Nicholas Postgate – written, as it is, by a contemporary who knew him well, speaks of him thus:

Sweet his behaviour, grave his speech,
He did by good example teach;
His love right bent, his will resign'd
Serene his look and calm his mind:
His sanctity to that degree,
As angels live, so lived he.

Even in its days of baroque exuberance, the Catholic Faith has always been fundamentally a simple Faith. In times of persecution the lack of visual support has made this simplicity doubly eloquent. Stripped of all, save heart and core, the underground Church turns solely to the Person of Jesus Christ, God and Man – Christ and his Cross; and is at the same time sustained by the realization of the Communion of Saints and the assurance of Resurrection. If the Church on Earth seems at times to be overcome by the forces of the world which resent it, the awareness that the Church Militant is in itself only a part of the Church Suffering and the Church Triumphant becomes strikingly relevant.

It is only in this context that we can venture to approach the profound simplicity of the Postgate Hymn and the man who composed it. This enables us to 'grasp' the 'serene' look, the 'calm' mind, the 'love right bent' and the 'will resigned' of Nicholas Postgate – the heart orientated to God-made-Man; the expression of an infinite love; the horror of sin; the confidence in God's mercy; the joy, even in adversity, of Christian living; the efficacy of grace despite the 'weight of flesh and blood'; the tranquillity which seeks eternity.

If we look hard, we find in these simple lines the essence of the Faith and a living picture of the Christ-centred devotion of the Martyr of the Moors. We find, too, the warm, simplicity that emanates from the Scriptures. Nothing ponderous. A delicate lightness of touch, whereby the writer, evoking the dove sent out from the Ark by Noe, sees as his sole support, his sole resting place, the outstretched hand of God.

The Trial

The depositions taken at Brompton having been forwarded to York, the trial of Nicholas Postgate took place at the Lent Assizes in 1679, in the Guildhall where Margaret Clitherow had been tried and condemned in 1586.

The building, which backs on to the Ouse below Lendal Bridge, is approached from Lendal Street under the archway. It dates from 1378. In 1942 it was severely damaged in an air-raid, but has since been painstakingly restored to its medieval appearance.

The official records of the trial being no longer extant, the precise date is not known. It must have been sometime between 7 March and 26 March; on the former day the deposition of Richard Morrice was taken at Brompton, while on the latter John Ryther, a Catholic gentleman living at Scarcroft in the West Riding, wrote in a letter to a friend, Richard Towneley of Towneley Hall (a centre of Catholic life in Lancashire): 'Old Mr Poskett is found guilty as being a priest.' Mr Ryther goes on to say that the judge was 'civil' and implies that some think the gaoler too easy-going. All sources make it clear that Postgate was charged not with involvement in the Titus Oates plot, but under the statute of 1585 (27 Elizabeth 1.2) against 'Jesuits, seminary priests . . .'

According to one account, quoted by Dom Bede Camm in *Forgotten Shrines*, 'the Judge, like a scarletted huntsman', cheered on the hounds in pursuit of the quarry. It is, however, generally agreed, that in fact the judge was in sympathy with his prisoner, refusing as long as possible to accept that his priesthood was proven – the one person who could prove it being the prisoner himself or someone who had been present at his ordination. According to John Knaresborough, writing in 1710 (he was seven years old when Nicholas Postgate was executed), the judge was most 'civil' and would gladly have acquitted the prisoner. The evidence, however, of Elizabeth Wood, Elizabeth Baxter and Richard Morrice – all of whom claimed to have seen him baptize, marry, and bury the dead, prevailed over any wish of the Judge to show mercy. The prisoner was convicted by the jury and sentenced to death.

Only once did he lose his composure. It was when a woman, one of his own converts to whom he had shown particular kindness, bore witness against him. The injustice cut him to the quick. For a moment his lips quivered, tears came to his eyes.

As to the barbarous death that awaited him – not even this could quench his gentle humour. Had he not cause, he asked, to be thankful to the Judge in that he had been granted 'a short-cut' to heaven?

The legal men dispersed to enjoy a bottle of wine.

The prisoner returned to his cell in the Castle.

Scarcely had he done so when the woman who had testified against him, who had brought tears to his eyes, came to him, weeping in remorse, to beg his pardon. He blessed her, calmed her, and gave her some money that had been given by friends to provide for him such comforts as it could; it would pay, he told her, her journey home.

Postgate remained a prisoner in the Castle for more than four months. By favour of the Judge who had condemned him, all who wanted to visit him were allowed to do so. He received them with the 'open arms of charity'. Otherwise, he prayed, and, when it was possible, he said Mass.

The Point of Departure

He, whose entire life had been a preparation for death, made his last-minute preparation – like a traveller on the point of departure.

In consequence of the Titus Oates plot, priests were being condemned to death, then in many instances left lingering in prison, the authorities being uncertain as to the wisdom of executing persons in vast numbers who in the majority of cases had done nothing to merit such a penalty. Then on 11 July 1679, the Privy Council issued instructions concerning 'diverse Popish priests who have been condemned in several counties: it was this day ordered by their Lordships in Council that the respective Judges who go the circuits where the said priests remain do forthwith give direction that they be executed according to law'.

During July and August there was what one can only call a country-wide massacre. Apart from Nicholas Postgate there were put to death six priests in England and

Wales: John Plessington, at Chester; Philip Evans and John Lloyd at Cardiff; John Wall at Worcester; John Kemble at Hereford; David Lewis at Usk, Monmouthshire. William Lloyd died in prison at Brecon.

The Last Day

The seventh day of August was appointed for the death of Nicholas Postgate.

Early that morning two women, as well as other visitors, came to see him; Mrs Fairfax, wife of Charles Fairfax of York, and Mrs Meynell of Kilvington, after making their confession, begged his blessing and proceeded to take leave of him. Incidentally, Postgate who at all times was primarily a pastoral priest did not allow politics to influence him. There is no evidence that he was interested in politics. Of these two women Mrs Meynell had married into a Royalist family, one of whose members had been killed while fighting at Pontefract; Mrs Fairfax, into the family of the Parliamentary leader who had been Governor of York.

This last meeting was for the two women an occasion of deep distress. Postgate, on the other hand gave no sign of disquiet, no sign of distress; he was, to all appearances, in good spirits. 'Cheerful' was the word used by John Knaresborough to whom Mrs Meynell recounted the happenings of that last morning. Postgate came up to the two women, both of whom were pregnant, and laying his right hand on one, his left on the other, he said: 'Be of good cheer, children! You will both be delivered of sons.'

The happenings of that morning were related to John Knaresborough by Mrs Fairfax on 5 October 1705 in her own home in the presence of her niece, 'the widdow Briggham'. She also gave him a piece of cloth dipped in Mr Postgate's blood by a servant present at his death.

Nicholas Postgate wore for his execution the little primitive crucifix, now at Ampleforth, and new clothes brought to him by his friends that he might 'enter as if to the nuptials of the Lamb in his wedding garment'. This was a tradition commonly observed among the martyrs. Whatever Postgate might have thought about the custom, it would have been out of character not to have shown appreciation of the attention shown by his friends. Not so Thomas More, who endured so much with unsurpassed courage and humour; he would have none of it – he was not willing to deck himself out in garments in which, when he was dead, his executioner, he said, would strut around.

Laid on a sledge Nicholas Postgate was dragged from the prison through the streets of York, along Castlegate, across the Ouse Bridge and through the Micklegate Bar. Then outside the city. Like his Master, he met his death outside the city walls. The place of execution, the Knavesmire, is to the west on the road to Tadcaster where the Race Course is today. It was a place of pilgrimage for Margaret Clitherow; she used to go there at night to pray at a spot hallowed by the blood of her fellow-Catholics. The gallows stood there from 1679 to 1812. The exact spot is marked by a simple stone block, bearing one word: Tyburn. It was put there in the year 1970.

Such spirit, such fortitude did Nicholas Postgate show, over eighty years old though he was, that the journey to the place of execution was said to resemble a triumphal procession rather than the passage of a condemned man to his death. Catholics and Protestants escorted him on his way, the latter, no less than the former, marvelling at his courage and mourning his fate.

It was customary before an execution for the victim to address the spectators – those who had come whether to honour him or to mock. Some of the speeches were surprisingly long. Possibly the effort to compose a speech, coupled with an only human satisfaction in being able, if possible, to deliver it well, may have provided a much needed distraction. Be that as it may, it was taken for granted that every prospective martyr would deliver immediately before his death an oration protesting his innocence and justifying his Catholicism. (Richard Langhorne, a barrister in the Inner Temple, composed a long meditation in verse.) According to an eye witness an immense crowd stood in complete silence, when, on 20 June 1679, the 'five holy Jesuits' as Thomas Ward calls them, spoke at Tyburn for not less than an hour each, denying having had any part whatsoever in the Popish plot. After that, John Gavan, outstanding among the five for his cool courage, led them in a collective act of contrition.

The veteran John Wall, immediately before being executed, apologized for his inability, through sheer physical weakness, to deliver a speech; he had, he said, given his oration to a friend to be printed.

Nicholas Postgate's final words were brief, for whereas his courage was boundless his physical strength was fast failing. He was dying, he said, for the Catholic Faith, not for any plot but for his religion. He asked the Sheriff, (who, as the principal agent of the Crown, was present at executions), to assure the King that he had never at any time wronged his Majesty in any way whatsoever. He prayed God, he said, to grant to the King grace and the light of truth. Finally, he declared that he forgave all who had done wrong to himself and brought him to his death, and desired, for himself, forgiveness from all.

The importance of this practice lies in the fact, John Kenyon has noted in *The Popish Plot*, that the victims did not on any occasion acknowledge their guilt, although they were offered pardon 'in return for a full confession, or any confession at all'.

When Nicholas Postgate prayed that the King might receive 'grace and the light of truth' did he know that, in all but outward observances, Charles II was already little short of being the Catholic he was to become on his death-bed in 1685? We cannot say. As compared with today, communication was difficult. Nevertheless, tongues wag. And rumour, whether it be based on fact or fiction, if it concerns persons in high places, spreads with incredible speed.

What Postgate would not have known is that in this same year, 1679, Charles snatched from the hands of Sir William Waller, unsurpassed as a 'priest-taker', a crucifix containing a fragment of the True Cross and wore it until the day he died, when he handed it to his brother, the Duke of York.

Nor did Postgate live long enough to know that Charles, during his last years, when he entered the Queen's boudoir (Queen Catherine bore witness to this), used to turn to the portraits of those same 'five holy Jesuits' (as Thomas Ward calls them, in his poem *The English Reformation*), to whose execution the King had for reasons of expediency shamefully consented in the summer of 1679, kiss their hands and beg their forgiveness.

One would like to know, too, whether Charles had any inkling that the eighty-two-year-old priest, executed outside the walls of York, was the same priest who in 1649 had visited his father Charles I in Pickering Castle: that in April 1642 this same priest, then in the prime of life, was chaplain to the Hungate family at Saxton, a short way from Bootham Bar where Charles I, along with his son, now Charles II, was staying at the Manor House.

Having spoken his last words, Nicholas Postgate gave himself up to his executioner. He was hanged, cut down, disembowelled and quartered in accordance with the sentence passed on him.

The ground was stained with his blood.

What remained of his body was given to friends for burial, and taken away on a four-wheeled cart. Catholics and non-Catholics accompanied it to the place of burial.

His clothes and other possessions were bought at an exaggerately high price. For many of the details we are indebted to John Warner, S.J., and John Knaresborough. According to the latter there was enclosed in the coffin a copper plate bearing the words:

> Here lyeth that Rd and pious divine Dr Nicholas Postgate, who was educated in the English College at Doway. And after he had labour'd fifty years (to the admirable benefit and conversion of hundrd [*sic*] of souls) was at last advanced to a glorious crown of martyrdom at the city of York on the seventh of August 1679, having been a priest 51 years, aged 82.

Where he is buried is unknown.

In the *Douai Diaries* the word 'Martyr' is inserted after his name.

8

THE POSTGATE TRADITION

The 'Cultus'

'One can only conclude that Nicholas Postgate was a very special person'.

These words are from a letter written to me in November 1979, by a Mrs Mary Noble of Kendal, who during the twenties had spent much of her childhood at Glaisdale, seven miles from Egton Bridge, and at Ugthorpe where her mother was headmistress of the school until she retired in 1941.

'Very special'. The thought was prompted by the fact, verified by old records, that, as well as Nicholas Postgate, there were from time to time other priests in the same area. Yet it is he who stands out, he who is remembered; not so much perhaps as one of the 'glorious band of martyrs', which indeed he is, as because he was kindly, humorous, reassuring – so much so that to console a penitent he would admit his own failings.

Christ-like Humility

Again, in doing good he was unobtrusive, not simply because in penal times it was dangerous for a priest to be in the limelight. Such was his nature; he was humble in the true, Christ-like sense of that much misused word.

That he should have been passed over (he and one Irish Franciscan) when Pope Pius XI, in 1929, beatified those executed as a result of the Titus Oates conspiracy, was, as John Keynon has noted in *The Popish Plot*, 'inexplicable'. Yes, 'inexplicable', but not inappropriate; in life Nicholas Postgate had never been thrustful.

No wonder people had not only welcomed him but sought him out. No wonder they had come to see him while he was in prison in York, had accompanied him to the place of execution and followed his body to the graveside.

No wonder he left behind, when he died, not so much an illustrious name as an aura of gentleness, tranquillity, peace.

What may be called the Postgate *cultus* began on the day he died, when Catholics and Protestants alike followed his body to the grave. It has continued quietly, down to our own times. In 1979 at a rally at Egton Bridge in a field beyond St Hedda's Church – Nicholas Postgate's birthplace across the hedge – I was impressed, I remember, by a group of teenagers standing, a few yards away, throughout the Mass, motionless, engrossed.

The preacher, Fr Roland Connelly, reminded us that, when Postgate was tramping the moors, there was not in those days a Catholic church in England open to the public. Barns were used as chapels, attics as churches, the moor as a vast cathedral. The priest, in those times, 'lurked rather than lived', aware that a smile could conceal a traitor, an innocent question an informer.

Keeping Memory Alive

'I remember', the preacher at the rally went on, 'as a small boy at Ugthorpe, listening to such vivid stories about Father Postgate that I expected him to walk in at any moment. The people of the moors have long memories, and before the blast furnaces of Teesside robbed them of their silence and the blare of television drowned the quiet voice of the storyteller, the long conversations by the fireside on winter evenings kept Postgate's memory alive.'

'Ould Nick'

Mrs Noble recalls a similar gathering at Ugthorpe some years back when a sudden downpour soaked everyone as they stood in the open field. Then the following year, when there was a gathering at Egton Bridge, the sun was shining. However, Hedda, an elderly friend of Mrs Noble and her family, was taking no risks; he stood there well buttoned up in his raincoat. 'Don't you trust Father Postgate?' Mrs Noble's husband asked him, glancing at the sky. 'Thou knows ould Nick as well as I do!' was Hedda's sardonic reply. This is typical of the warm affection in which Father Postgate is held among his own people, as though he were still in their midst.

This Hedda is better known as Hedda Watson, a devout member of the Ancient Guild of St Joseph and St Hedda, and a tremendous admirer of Father Postgate. In 1977 he composed the following prayer.

> You knew our forefathers, and you knew the things we care about – our way of life. Our fields and paths you trod, and knew too well dark, misty, stormy Blackamoor. You died that we might keep the faith you taught. Do not desert us, for once again our world is all awry and we perplexed. Priest of the Moorland, pray for us.

Nicholas Postgate was fond of children. They used to visit him on Blackamoor. And long afterwards – it is still so today – children continued to show interest in him. The mother of a moorland family writes:

> As children we had the idea that Father Postgate was the priest immediately before Father Rigby, who at Ugthorpe had built the school back in the eighteen hundreds. The old folks in Ugthorpe used to talk about 'Father Rigby's time'. Then as the years went by Father Rigby, we noticed, seemed to fade out. But not Father Postgate. He was still spoken of by the ordinary folk all over the area. To us he was completely real.
>
> Gradually we learned his story, heard about the Mass House and the relics. In several homes there were crosses made from wood said to have come from places associated with him, especially the Mass House. These crosses, I remember, were quite plain, about nine or ten inches tall, standing on a plinth – no figure on them. Other small objects were made from this same wood, especially by a Mr Will Ward who lived in the district. One of these was a missal stand, now in the church at Sleights. When this small church was first opened at the junction of the village road and the road to Ugglebarnby, people from the moors, mostly non-Catholics, came to the priest, Fr Gannon, bringing all sorts of things, candle-sticks, cloths and so on. 'These', they would say, 'belonged to Father Postgate'.

In the summer of 1979 children were in the forefront when *High Courage*, a play based on the latter years of Father Postgate's life was performed at St Francis School, Acklam, Middlesbrough.

Written originally for adults by Sister Mary Cecily of the Sisters of Mercy, an authority on Nicholas Postgate, it was adapted for children and produced by Mrs Jane Lecky of St Francis School. It made a remarkable impact. Parties coming from surprising distances were delighted by the colourful scenes – the effect heightened by appropriate music, singing and dancing. The eleven-year-old boy who played Nicholas Postgate combined dignity with a delightful humour. Particularly impressive was the interpretation of Sir William Cayley (Justice of the Peace at Brompton) by an Indian boy. Moreover, thanks to the guidance of Mgr Canon Peter Storey, Vicar General, historical accuracy was observed.

The audience who joined spontaneously in the singing of the Postgate Hymn included persons living in the area whose forebears had been involved in Postgate's life.

There is no question of Nicholas Postgate's personality's being forgotten.

The Postgate Centre, founded at Endsleigh Training College, Hull, in 1951, where much work is still done to further his cause, was transferred to St Hedda's Church, Egton Bridge, in 1965. In the first year there it was visited by more than 900 people in organized pilgrimages or coming individually, attracted by the relics on display and by the nearby Mass House. One visitor was the Rt Revd Wm. Gordon Wheeler, Bishop of Leeds. Another was Fr Philip Caraman, S.J., the well-known writer on English recusants.

In 1977 when a new road was made through the village of Ugthorpe the local Council, although few if any Catholics were serving on it, decided to call it Postgate Way.

In *The Universe* of 5 October 1973 there was a photograph of 'The Postgate' public house at Egton Bridge.

The devotion takes many forms. Every year a Methodist whose home was in Middlesbrough used to make a pilgrimage from there on foot to Egton Bridge.

Another non-Catholic, Mr Graham Leach of Sandsend, near Whitby, when he made a picture map of the district, put in Nicholas Postgate near the windmill at Ugthorpe. As, except for Captain Cook, there was no other figure shown on the map, Mr Leach was asked why he had included Postgate. 'Of all local worthies,' he replied, 'Father Postgate seems to be most like Christ. Knowing that a price was on his head although he had committed no crime, knowing, still more, that his death was unjust, his trial a farce, he never spoke a bitter word.'

Postgate the Catholic priest, and Cook the Protestant mariner had more in common than is at first apparent. Great Ayton where Cook went to school is some five miles from Guisborough where the road strikes across the moors to Whitby. Both were men of vigour, determination, courage; both died a violent death, Cook in 1777 nearly a hundred years after Postgate. The words below the statue of Captain Cook looking out over the sea at Whitby, 'To strive, to seek, to find and not to yield', are no less applicable to the priest.

Yes, Nicholas Postgate was, and is, a real person not only to Catholics but to non-Catholics. Hence what Mrs Noble calls the 'easy interaction', the 'ecumenical' spirit at Ugthorpe between the two churches, Catholic and Protestant, the two communities. 'They worked together,' she says, 'played together, yet stuck to their differences, each respecting the other. A few Irish priests who came in the thirties did not know what to make of it. They found it a "right puzzle", yet they learnt to live with it and enjoy it.'

His chalice, Mrs Noble continues, was used regularly at Ugthorpe, until just before World War II, when Fr Currie, the priest at that time, decided to keep it for special occasions because the screw-thread was wearing and making the chalice unsteady; he did not want to have the three separate parts made into one.

'We used to hear, too,' she goes on, 'how Nicholas Postgate spread out the sheets, to show he was going to say Mass. In our day it was perfectly credible because in the thirties it was still the custom for people to spread their washing on hedges to dry. So in Father Postgate's day the sheets would have had meaning for "those in the know" and wouldn't have attracted unwanted attention.'

A thing that impressed Mrs Noble as a child was the fact that a man of his advanced years was able to look after so large an area: 'We children didn't realize that we knew only a mere corner of his "parish"! We used to walk pretty often from Glaisdale to Egton Bridge for Mass and from Glaisdale to Ugthorpe. The roads and paths were rougher in the 1920s than they are today. How much rougher, then, and more desolate they must have been in the 1600s! And the winters! In the 1920s we were snowed up at some point every year, sometimes for days, sometimes for weeks. Nowadays bulldozers and helicopters come to the rescue. In the thirties man-power and shovels were our only resources.'

Vanished Landmarks

Think then what it must have been like in the time of Nicholas Postgate. Think of the moors – a great, white wasteland. Hedgerows and landmarks vanished. Houses robbed of their familiar outlines!

The *cultus* of Nicholas Postgate was at first confined mainly to his own area. Naturally so, when it was difficult to get from place to place. A sudden interest, however, 'took-off' after World War II when the Teessiders, in consequence of the increase in motor-cars and buses, found that the moors were, so to speak, on their doorsteps.

At Pickering he was remembered with special devotion, thanks largely to Fr Edward H. Bryant, a convert to Catholicism who died in 1937. The signature of Nicholas Postgate was reproduced on the Parish Magazine. Pilgrims were encouraged; a party came from Scarborough, it is recorded in the magazine, in an open wagonette on a day of rain and wild wind.

When Fr Bryant built his permanent church in Pickering in 1911 he inserted in the altar Postgate's square slate which he used to take on his travels as an altar-stone. Crowds of people wrote asking to be remembered in intercessions to the Martyr. Fr Quinlan tells how at some time in the fifties a certain Lawrence Carter, over eighty years old, recalled that when he was a boy he used to be given these petitions to put on the altar table and that it was covered thick with them. Furthermore, in 1959, when the altar was being repaired and the back had to be removed, quantities of similar petitions were found inside.

Across the border in Lancashire, research, for which we are indebted to J. C. H. Aveling, into parochial documents in the County Record Office at Preston brought to light a parchment-covered notebook which described the building of the Catholic chapel at nearby Hindley in the year 1780. It gave a list of 'Persons applying to be Cured of their Maladies by the touch of the Hand of the Revd Nicholas Postgate'. The list consists of several pages made out in columns, giving dates, names, comments. Some 200 entries were made between October 1850 and March 1853.

The Hand at Ampleforth

This hand, now at Ampleforth, was at Hindley an object of pilgrimage. People came, three or four a day, to make petitions – from Liverpool, Manchester, Wigan, Bolton; from Leeds, Bradford, Huddersfield. A few gave London addresses, others addresses in Ireland. That is not to say they had come this distance for this precise purpose; they could have been employed in the North and have given their home addresses.

The following are instances of non-Catholics:

'June 15th, 1851, Richard Garbutt, Chorley, Fitts. Protestant. Better.'
'June 24th, 1851, Ann Cotton, N. R. Brownedge, Preston. St Vitus Dance. Protestant. Cured.' This is the only case where the word 'cured' is added.

The hand at Ampleforth is revered. Cardinal Hume, Archbishop of Westminster and formerly Abbot of Ampleforth, took this hand with him from Yorkshire to St Joseph's Hospice, Hackney, when he went there to bless a sick boy. The boy did not want to become a Catholic, then changed his mind and before he died asked to be received into the Church. Several of his relations also became Catholics. His Eminence added that the two things, the hand and the change of religion, were not of necessity connected.

Epilogue

'It is the Mass that matters.'

The words are those of Augustine Birrell, the Nonconformist scholar. 'It is the Mass', he goes on, 'that makes the difference, so hard to define, so subtle is it yet so perceptible, between a Catholic country and a Protestant one, between Dublin and Edinburgh, between Havre and Cromer.' (*The Collected Essays and Addresses*, vol. ii, pp. 345–6.)

It is the Mass that gives to the life of Nicholas Postgate its distinctive quality. It is the significance of the oratory hidden under the thatch at Egton. It is the significance of his death – his death as a priest.

To emphasize what his priesthood means let me recall a dialogue that took place in the year 1614, six years before Nicholas Postgate entered the English College at Douai, between a Benedictine priest, Blessed Maurus Scott, and Dr John King, Protestant Bishop of London.

'Are you a priest?', the Bishop asked.

'My Lord,' Maurus replied, 'let me ask you, are *you* a priest?'

'No,' said the prelate.

'No priest, no bishop.'

'I am a priest, but not a massing priest.'

'If you are a priest, you are a sacrificing priest, for sacrifice is essential to priesthood, and if you are a sacrificing priest you are a massing priest – for it is one and the same.'

The 'bishop' continued to say that he was not a massing priest.

'If you are no massing priest you are no sacrificing priest; if no sacrificing priest, no priest at all, and therefore no bishop.'

In response to this, Maurus Scott was put to death. His body was retrieved not by his fellow countrymen but by a group of devoted Spaniards.

Like Maurus Scott, Nicholas Postgate died for the Mass; not for ritual and ceremony in general, but for sacrifice – the sacrifice made once and for all, for us men and for our salvation, on Calvary, and at the same time the closest bond possible on earth between God and man, man and his fellowmen.

The Mass, this *mysterium fidei*, gave to Nicholas Postgate, when he was an old man, the impetus to tramp the moors to feed God's people and his own, the strength, too, to die with dignity and lightness of heart.

The Mass does not change. And fundamentally there is little difference between the moors of the 1500s and the moors we know today: the purple glow of ling; a sudden daub of emerald; cotton-grass trembling in the breeze; a grey solitary cross; contented black-faced sheep; an all-enveloping numinous silence that lifts the heart from time into eternity.

'All is always now.'

The Mass is the Mass. The moors are the moors. Nicholas Postgate is Nicholas Postgate. Would it be surprising were he to come striding across the turf, his brown tunic and white cape stirring in the wind, a staff in his hand, a distant gaze in the clear blue eyes? Would he not greet me as one of his own? And would I not greet him in return?

It is hard to overestimate the impact that environment can make upon us.

Teilhard de Chardin's *Le Milieu Divin* would not be the book it is if he had not as a boy roamed with his father the rugged countryside of Sarcenat, searching for zoological and mineral specimens, in an area rich in insect life and flowers, in sight of rounded volcanic hills, in sound of murmuring streams.

Wuthering Heights would not be the work with which we are familiar if Emily Brontë had spent her childhood in Halifax instead of at her father's parsonage at Haworth. At one time when Emily was away from home Charlotte feared that her delicate, highly sensitive sister would die if she were not brought back to her beloved moors.

As to Nicholas Postgate, if our knowledge of his personality is somewhat scanty, I have said enough, I hope, to show that the moors contributed to the man he was. Bearing in mind other facets of his life, other influences, we may still call his spirituality a moorland one.

Those long apostolic journeys through the ling or the snow, the wide horizons, the opal sky – must they not have prompted a realization of that inward journey, that return to the centre of our being where God dwells? For, as well as having made us 'in his own image', is he not himself the very ground of our existence both by nature and by grace?

And why not also consider Postgate and the moors in reverse? Is it merely fanciful to think that these same moors of North-east Yorkshire have, thanks to him, taken on a new light, assumed an additional dimension? I do not think so.

On the contrary, I am of the opinion of T. S. Eliot, as expressed in *Murder in the Cathedral*, that wherever a saint has made his dwelling, wherever a martyr has shed his blood, there the ground is for ever holy. The same poet, reflecting on the life of prayer led at Little Gidding in the seventeenth century by Nicholas Ferrar and his community, reminds us of those countless places 'where prayer has been valid'—places immortalized by the prayer of those who have gone before. For prayer, like music when the melody has ended, still lingers in the memory.

We have, each one of us, our choice, whether it be the Church of the Holy Sepulchre at Jerusalem, or Walsingham, or Bylands Abbey.

For myself I like to think of that strange, intangible peace, incapable of being destroyed by any intrusion of pilgrims or tourists, that St Cuthbert bestowed, all those years ago, upon wave-lashed Lindisfarne and the storm-tossed Northumbrian coast: the peace, likewise, that St Columba bestowed on desolate Farne where – his biographer, Adamnan, tells us – his bed was a rock, his pillow a stone, his soup the diluted leaves of nettles.

Nicholas Postgate, too, was a man of prayer.

As he travelled the vast silent moors, in sunlight, in starlight, in rain, in wind, in ice and snow, did he not see, as St John of the Cross saw, traces of God's own self left upon creation?

Did he murmur or cry out for joy:

Benedicite sol et luna
Benedicite stellae caeli
Benedicite omnes venti
Benedicite pruinae et nives
Benedicite lux et tenebrae.

Blessed be the sun and moon
Blessed be the stars of heaven
Blessed be all the winds

Blessed be the frost and snow
Blessed be light and darkness.

Blessed Nicholas Postgate, teach us to pray.
Teach us to glorify God in his creation.
Teach us to find him in the depth of our own being.

INDEX OF PLACES

Acklam, 76
Ampleforth Abbey, 51 52 69 80 81
Arras, 20

Biggin House, 41 50 60
Blackamoor, Blackamor, 14 37 39 52 75
Bootham Bar, 26 42 71
Bridgeholme, 41 42
Bridgeholme Green, 26 42
Brompton, 39 54 59 60 65 66 77
Bylands Abbey, 84

Danby, 34
Danby Castle, 36
Devil's Dump, 61
Douai, ix 4 7 12 13 14 15 16 17 18 20 21 22 24 26 27 29 31 40 41 46 55 58 72 81

Egton, 1 10 11 13 14 24 34 39 41 47 48 50 55 81
Egton Bridge, 1 2 10 11 12 14 26 27 32 39 47 48 49 52 55 62 73 74 75 77 79
Egton High Moor, 52
Esk, the river, 1 12 52 53 61
Eskdale, 36 39
Eskdaleside, 57
Everingham, 26 27 28

Farndale, 35
Fylingdales Moor, 52 53

Glaisdale, 1 11 73 79
Goathland, 11 52 53
Goathland Moors, 1 39
Grosmont, 1 24 39 48 52 53 61
Guisborough, 34 39 41 53 78

Halsham, 26
Helmsley, 13
Hindley, 80
Holderness, 26
Hole of Horcum, 53
Hull, 27 77
Hutton-le-Hole, 48

Kilvington, 51 68
Kilvington Castle and Kilvington Hall, 27
Knavesmire, the, 2 26 64 69

Leeds, 13 80
Leighton, 24
Littlebeck, 45 55
Lythe, 11

Middlesbrough, ix 76 77
Mulgrave and Mulgrave Castle, 24 36 37 52

Old Elvet, 51
Osmotherley, 39
Our Lady of Mount Grace, shrine of, 39

Pickering, 39 52 53 54 59 79 80

Rheims, 16 18

Saxton, 25 26 28 71
Scarborough, 23 26 54 59 60 79
Scarcroft, 66
Sleights, 1 39 61 76
Staithes, 23

Tadcaster, 25 69
Thirsk, 23 26 27 61
Towton, 24
Tyburn i. London, 5 6 18 57 70
ii. York, 69

Ugglebarnby, 12 55 61 76
Ugthorpe, 33 34 38 39 42 43 47 51 52 53 60 61 73 74 75 76 77 78 79
Upsall Castle, 24

Wakefield, 7 13
Whitby, 1 10 12 22 23 33 34 35 39 44 48 49 53 54 56 57 60 61 77 78

York, 2 5 7 9 15 19 20 22 23 24 25 26 27 42 43 50 51 55 60 62 65 65–72 74